MW00773733

"Authors Warren Trest and Don Dodd have produced a superbly researched and written account of one of the darkest tragedies of the Cold War era. *Wings of Denial* describes in chilling detail the bloody impact of President John F. Kennedy's personal intervention in the Cuban exile invasion plan, and the doomed attempt by a handful of courageous Alabama Air Guardsmen to carry out that fatally flawed plan. More troubling still is the Kennedy Administration's use of the CIA as a scapegoat for the failure, a cynical act of political expediency that successfully buried the truth about the Bay of Pigs invasion for decades after that dreadful day in April 1961."

> —COL. MICHAEL E. HAAS, USAF, RET., author, *Apollo's Warriors: U.S. Air Force Special Operations During the Cold War*

"Trest and Dodd provide remarkable new insight into one of America's most secret military operations, the failed April 1961 Bay of Pigs invasion. Expertly written, using heretofore classified documents and interviews with the participants, the authors have crafted a well-deserved and heartfelt testimony to the patriotism and bravery of the Alabama Air National Guardsmen who paid the ultimate price for their country."

> — TIMOTHY N. CASTLE, Ph.D., Associate Professor, Air War College, Maxwell AFB, Alabama

". . . a well-written and informative account of the covert role played by Alabama Air National Guardsmen—employed by the CIA as civilian contract personnel—in the abortive Bay of Pigs invasion. It sheds new light on the Air Guard's hard-to-document involvement in the murky world of clandestine operations."

> — CHARLES J. GROSS, Ph.D., chief, Air National Guard History/National Guard Bureau

Bay of Pigs display at the Southern Museum of Flight,
Birmingham, Alabama

WINGS

OF

DENIAL

The Alabama Air National Guard's
Covert Role at the Bay of Pigs

WARREN TREST
AND DON DODD

NewSouth Books
Montgomery

TO THOSE WHO SERVED

NewSouth Books
P.O. Box 1588
Montgomery, AL 36104

Library of Congress Cataloging-in-Publication Data

Trest, Warren A.
Wings of denial : the Alabama Air National Guard's covert role at
the Bay of Pigs / Warren Trest and Don Dodd.
p.cm.
Includes bibliographical references (p.) and index.
ISBN 1-58838-021-1
1. Cuba—History—Invasion, 1961—Aerial operations. 2.
Alabama. Air National Guard. 3. United States. Central Intelligence Agency. I. Dodd, Don. II. Title.

F1788 .T74 2001
972.9106'4--dc21

2001030168

Design by Randall Williams
Printed in the United States of America by Victor Graphics

Contents

Preface

FOR FOUR DECADES the role that the Alabama Air National Guard played in the ill-fated Bay of Pigs invasion has been relegated to the footnotes of Cold War history. The Air Guard's role was not only hidden under a shroud of secrecy imposed on the covert operation by the CIA, but became lost in the Vietnam War's escalation after President Kennedy was assassinated in 1963. Also obscured in the sweep of Cold War history were enough broad parallels between the three-day battle at the Bay of Pigs and the protracted war in Vietnam to suggest that the former might be seen as a microcosm of the latter. Both were sideshows within the wider East-West confrontation, both were saddled with "no-win" strategies, and both were doomed by the politics of indecision.

For the Alabama guardsmen and their comrades who were involved with the Bay of Pigs, the ghosts were no less haunting than those that followed us home from the war in Vietnam. They believed just as deeply in the rightness of their mission, and in the need to do their mission right. Getting to know these forgotten men was the high point in doing the research for this book on the Air Guard's covert role in the invasion. Their memories are as fresh and their patriotic spirits are as high as they were forty years ago when they volunteered to help the CIA-backed Cuban exiles in their fight for freedom. This book could not have been written without their cooperation.

The authors are indebted to Dr. J. Dudley Pewitt, the board of directors, and the staff at the Southern Museum of Flight in Birmingham, Alabama, for their unstinting support of the project. Joe Shannon, a board member and Bay of Pigs veteran, deserves special mention. He gave freely of his time and was an invaluable source of information throughout the project. We also greatly appreciate the receptivity, congeniality, and helpfulness of other Bay of Pigs participants who consented to interviews and provided us with valuable information: Bill Bainbridge, Bill Baker, Willie Colvert, Dan Crocker, Edward Ferrer, Bill Fultz, James Glenn, Bill Gray, James Harrison, Lou Hudson, Fred Raley, Robert L. Scoggins, Bob Stanley, John O. Spinks, Carl N. Sudano, L.D. Thomas, Bob Whitley, Roy Wilson, and Charles Yates.

We extend a special word of thanks to Amy Bartlett-Dodd who proofread, word-processed, and edited the interviews with participants. Amy and the friendly folks at the Bay of Pigs Museum in Miami also guided the authors to new research avenues on the internet. All of the Birmingham Public Library Research librarians were helpful, including Yvonne Crumpler, Jim Pate, and Mary Beth Newbill, as were Public Library personnel in Montgomery. The professional assistance the authors received from Joe Caver, Dennis Case, Heather Gilley, Essie Roberts, and Milton Steele with the USAF Historical Research Agency at Maxwell AFB was invaluable. Stephanie Harmon and Donna Billingsley at Maxwell's Air University Library provided valuable assistance, as did Dr. Marty Oliff, in charge of special collections at the Auburn University Library. Frazine Taylor graciously assisted with research at the Alabama Department of Archives and History.

We also greatly appreciate the help of Colonel Mike Haas (USAF, Ret.), Captain Edward Ferrer, and Janet Ray Weininger in providing documents and photographs. John Trest made a special contribution by producing maps for the book. Tom Trest assisted with research. Air National Guard historian Dr. Charles J. Gross and his staff in Washington, along with Don Gainor at Alabama Air National Guard headquarters in Montgomery provided useful information on General Doster's service as commander. The authors are grateful to all who shared their insights about the Alabama Air Guard's participation in the Cuban invasion. Thanks to their knowledge, the book is better informed than it otherwise would have been.

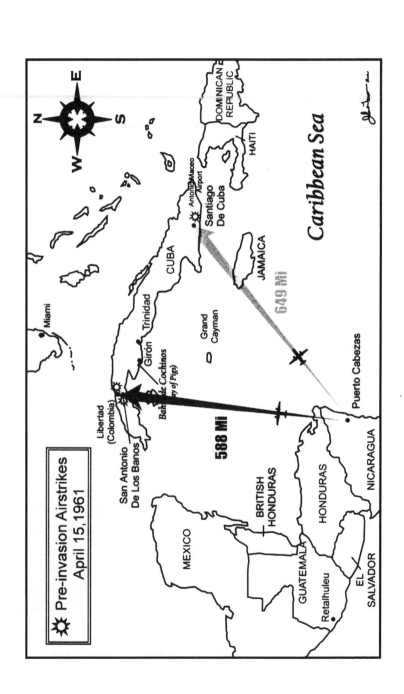

Pre-invasion Airstrikes April 15, 1961

Introduction

IN THE PREDAWN HOURS of April 19, 1961, six Douglas B-26 Invaders disguised with Cuban markings took off from a secret CIA base at Puerto Cabezas, Nicaraugua, and headed north over the moonlit waters of the Caribbean toward Cuba. Puerto Cabezas, known as "Happy Valley" to the pilots and crews, was the staging base for the ill-fated invasion at the Bay of Pigs. Armed to the teeth, the twin-engine B-26s flew the mission in two-ship formations—taking to the skies at 30-minute intervals to stagger their arrivals over the target area. The bombers were launched in a desperate attempt to stave off defeat for the brigade of Cuban exiles who were stranded on the embattled beachhead and fighting for their lives.[1]

For the first time during the invasion Alabama Air National Guard pilots were at the controls of warplanes taking part in the fray. Prior to April 19th the Alabama guardsmen were not allowed to fly combat missions in support of the brigade. The White House feared that an American pilot might be shot down and expose the U.S. Government's role in the covert affair. President John F. Kennedy, newly inaugurated and concerned about the political fallout from the invasion, was adamant that operations be carried

11

out in such a way that the U.S. Government could plausibly deny any involvement. Unfortunately, the concern for "plausible deniability" within the decision-making process took precedence over military requirements.[2]

Pre-invasion air strikes against Cuban airfields were held to a minimum to mask U.S. involvement. This was done on direct orders from the President. Remnants of Fidel Castro's air forces, including two British-built Sea Fury prop fighters and two Lockheed T-33 jet trainers with fighter capability, survived the attacks to strike back against the invasion forces and their limited air support. The fighters attacked the landing forces at will, sank their ammunition and supplies coming in from the sea, and wreaked havoc on the B-26s coming to their aid. The denial of U.S. fighter cover from the carrier *Essex* steaming offshore yielded command of the air to Castro's few surviving planes.

The minimal bombing strikes two days before the landing on April 17 not only failed to destroy all of Castro's planes, but alerted the Cuban dictator that the landing forces were on the way. On the morning of the 17th Castro's planes sank two of the brigade's ships, the *Houston* and the *Rio Escondido*, loaded with war supplies. Five of the liberation air force's 16 B-26s and their crews were lost on the day of the landing. Flying one and sometimes two missions a day— each mission six and one-half hours over open water without navigational aids—the Cuban pilots were physically and emotionally exhausted by the third day of the invasion. Air Guard Lieutenant Colonel Joseph L. Shannon recalled that the Cuban pilots were in no shape to fly on the 19th, but some flew anyway.[3]

Faced with exhausted aircrews and a desperate situation on the ground in Cuba, the CIA authorized Alabama guardsmen to fly missions on the 19th. Four Guard pilots and four crewmen stepped forward. The lead formation on the 19th was commanded by Billy "Dodo" Goodwin, a major in the Air Guard, and Gonzalo Herrera, a fearless Cuban pilot known as "El Tigre" by his compatriots. The other Alabama Guard pilots were Joe Shannon, Riley Shamburger, and Thomas Willard "Pete" Ray. Crew members from Alabama included Leo Francis Baker, Wade Gray, Carl "Nick" Sudano, and James Vaughn. A second exiled Cuban pilot, Mario Zuniga, and his observer rounded out the strike force.[4]

At the last minute the B-26s were promised air cover from the *Essex*, but in a tragic mix-up the jet fighters did not show until the bombers were leaving the target area. The Navy pilots had orders not to fire unless fired upon. When the unprotected bombers arrived over the beachhead at sunrise, the Cuban fighters were waiting for them. The two lead B-26s piloted by Goodwin and Herrera sustained hits but delivered their ordnance and were returning to Puerto Cabezas when the other bombers arrived in the target area. Two of the B-26s came under attack as they approached the beachhead. Joe Shannon was able to outmaneuver the T-33s, but his wingman Riley Shamburger was hit. Shamburger and his observer Wade Gray went down with their plane. Further inland, a Cuban fighter brought down Pete Ray's bomber as he pressed the attack against heavily defended targets. Ray and Leo Francis Baker, a flight engineer, survived the crash only to be killed in a shootout with Cuban soldiers.[5]

That afternoon the beachhead collapsed and the Cuban exiles, having exhausted their supplies and ammunition, surrendered to Castro's army. It had taken just seventy-two hours to crush the invasion. Some survivors were rescued by U.S. ships, but the brigade took heavy casualties including 114 men who died and 1,189 who were taken prisoner. Fidel Castro held the prisoners until December 1963 when he ransomed them to the United States for $53 million worth of food and drugs.[6] A humiliating defeat for the U.S. Government, the Bay of Pigs was a tragedy from which the Cuban exiles and their liberation movement would never recover.

No one shared the loss more than their U.S. comrades. Joe Shannon recalled that he and the other Alabama guardsmen had flown the final mission on 19 April because they "were closely associated with the Cuban aircrews, and . . . felt a strong dedication to their cause." Captain Edward B. Ferrer, a pilot in the liberation air force, wrote a book on the air battle at the Bay of Pigs and declared that the U.S. crews who volunteered to fly with them in combat were no longer advisers, but brothers.[7] Despite the swirl of controversy surrounding the Bay of Pigs fiasco and their strong feelings about the constraints placed on air power, Shannon and the other air guardsmen kept their silence for decades. They had been sworn to secrecy, and they honored that commitment. They did not even tell their wives.[8]

For the families of the four heroic guardsmen who gave their lives on the final day's mission, theirs was a compelling story. The families mourned their loss, but went years without knowing what happened to their loved ones. How could they relate the deaths to the Bay of Pigs if the government denied they were ever there? Some family members refused to give up. In a poignant twist to the Bay of Pigs tragedy the family of Pete Ray learned in 1978 that for 17 years his body had been refrigerated in Cuba on Castro's orders. The Castro regime kept the slain U.S. pilot's body as a propaganda trophy and as evidence that the U.S. government was behind the Bay of Pigs invasion.[9]

Thomas Ray, Jr., (a San Francisco attorney) and his sister Janet (the wife of an Air Force colonel and F-16 pilot) were small children when their father was killed. Although the family learned that he had died while supporting the invasion, officially he was never there. While growing up the son and daughter relentlessly pursued the truth about their father's death and what had happened to his body. The family's persistence persuaded the Cuban government to return Thomas Ray's body to Alabama for burial in December

1979. The U.S. Government finally admitted in May 1999, nearly four decades after the event, that Ray and three other Alabama guardsmen were shot down on April 19, 1961, flying combat over Cuba's Bahia de Cochinos.[10]

Over the past 40 years the daring B-26 mission on the final day of the invasion—resulting in the untimely death of four intrepid guardsmen—has become a symbol of the Alabama Air National Guard's role in the Bay of Pigs invasion. That role had its start when a large contingent of Alabama guardsmen, joined by other volunteers from Arkansas units and the civil aviation sector, deployed on a secret mission to Guatemala in late 1960. They served there as advisers to Cuban exiles who were preparing to liberate their homeland under the auspices of the CIA. No one else, not even their families, knew where they were.

The failure at the Bay of Pigs had far-reaching implications for the U.S. Government and its Cold War policies. It led directly to the Cuban missile crisis of 1962 and may have propagated the political indecision and myopia leading to our more tragic failure in the Vietnam War. For the Alabama Air National Guard there were no Bay of Pigs service medals or campaign streamers, but the experience has become a distinctive part of Air Guard history. For the guardsmen who were part of that history, their silence was a badge of honor. Their story begins on a crisp autumn morning in Birmingham, Alabama.

Going After 'the Bearded Lady'

O N THAT CRISP fall morning in October 1960 Brigadier General George Reid Doster had a curious visitor who came to Birmingham on a mission that would disrupt the daily routine of the Alabama Air National Guard and change the lives of air guardsmen under the general's command. The 42-year-old Doster, a burly cigar-chomping six-footer known as "Papa" to the troops, had been with the Alabama Air National Guard since the end of World War II. After the war he came home from the China-Burma-India Theater, made captain, and was assigned as the liaison officer for the Alabama Air Guard—giving him the distinction of being the first air guardsman in Alabama during the postwar period. Politically savvy and serving in the right place at the right time, Doster rose from captain to brigadier general in just over ten years. During the early 1960s, he was the man to see if you had business with the Air Guard and wanted to get an urgent mission done without too many questions being asked or without a mountain of red tape to climb.

From his headquarters on the north side of Birmingham's municipal airport, Doster commanded the 117th Tactical Reconnaissance Wing with flying units in both Birmingham and Montgomery, as well as Meridian, Mississippi, and Fort Smith, Arkansas. Alerted by the National Guard Bureau chief in Washington, D.C., to expect the unannounced visitor, the general's broad grin and bushy eyebrows concealed more than a little curiosity when the small, nondescript man walked into the outer office and identified himself as a government agent with the CIA. An expression of interest in what the man had to say creased Doster's brow when his uninvited guest revealed that the CIA wanted to recruit volunteers from the general's wing for a project of critical importance to the nation.[1]

Without going into details, the agent explained in a conspiratorial whisper that the CIA had a secret project in the works to arm and train a brigade of Cuban exiles for an invasion of their homeland. That the CIA had a plan to overthrow Fidel Castro was enough to demand the general's attention. The Cuban dictator had become a thorn in the side of the United States, a menace to his neighbors, and a threat to peace throughout the region. He was a cancer that needed to be removed. "So we're finally going after the bearded lady," was Doster's booming response.

The man threw Doster a quizzical look.

"Fidel. You know, the bearded lady," the general said. "You're finally going after that commie son of a bitch."

Continuing in a hushed voice, the man told Doster that the CIA had sent him to Birmingham to get the Alabama Guard's help in training Cuban exiles for the secret project. The agency planned to equip a small liberation air force with refurbished B-26 light bombers from the Air Force's mothball fleet at Davis-Monthan AFB in Tucson, Arizona. A cadre of experienced pilot instructors along with maintenance and armament crews was needed, and the CIA hoped to draw from the Alabama Guard's pool of proven resources. Having retired its B-26s in the late 1950s, the Birmingham wing was the last USAF unit to fly the WWII-vintage bombers.

Above: Before being retired in 1957 the B-26 Invader was the mainstay of the Alabama Air National Guard's 117th Tactical Reconnaissance Wing (Don Crocker Collection, Southern Museum of Flight).

Left: Brigadier General Reid Doster sits atop the cockpit of a B-26 bomber (courtesy of Colonel Mike Haas, USAF Ret.).

The agent asked if the general would be willing to recruit qualified volunteers to deploy to a secret base in Guatemala for an extended period. The men would be sheep-dipped (sanitized) and sworn to secrecy. They were to talk to no one, not even their families, about the mission.

"Mister, you got yourself an air force," Doster replied, jumping at the opportunity. "Nothing me and my boys would like better than to go down and kick Castro's butt." There was a second star in Doster's future whichever way he went, but an important mission like this one never hurt. It would also be good for "his boys" as he referred to the guardsmen in his wing. When the agent finished talking, Doster yelled to his secretary to get the governor's office on the telephone. When told that the governor would see them, Doster and the CIA man left in a staff car for the two-hour drive to Montgomery.

It was Reid Doster's favorite time of year. Alabama football was in the air and hunting season opened soon. The general was an avid outdoorsman who hated to be cooped up in an office. As they sped down U.S. Highway 31, early autumn colors enhanced the countryside of rolling hills, lazy pastures, patches of ravenous kudzu here and there, and groves of southern trees with their softly falling leaves. Everytime he traveled this route, which had become more frequently of late, Doster wished the state would hurry up and build the new interstate highway everyone was talking about.

The CIA man was quiet, a good listener. Doster was ebullient, talkative. He carried the conversation with good-old-boy talk mostly about hunting, fishing, and college football. His alma mater Auburn was still in the hunt for the Southeastern Conference championship, and he loved to tell anyone who would listen about it. Doster knew to stay clear of college football in their meeting with Governor John Patterson, however, because the chief executive was an alumnus of Auburn's traditional rival, the University of Alabama

Alabama Governor John Patterson, Brigadier General Reid Doster, and Lieutenant Colonel Joe Shannon. The governor presented Shannon's squadron with the Commander's Cup for 1960 (courtesy of Joe Shannon).

in Tuscaloosa. There was no need to push his luck with the governor.

Patterson received his two guests in the governor's mansion. The 22-room residence on South Perry Street, built at the turn of the century by the son of a former lieutenant governor and purchased by the State of Alabama in 1950, was an impressive structure. Patterson became the third governor to reside in the mansion when he took office in 1959. The governor was a warm and gracious host. Years later he recalled the two men coming to see him at the mansion and asking for his approval to recruit volunteers from the Alabama National Guard "to train Cubans in Guatemala for an invasion of Cuba." He was assured that the Alabama Guard would participate in a supporting role only and would not take an active part in the invasion. Patterson gave Doster the green light to involve the Alabama Guard within those parameters. [2]

The governor gathered from their discussion that the invasion was imminent, however, which gave him pause for thought. Since the meeting occurred in the heat of the presidential campaign between Kennedy and Nixon, Patterson feared that the Eisenhower Administration might be planning to invade Cuba before the election in hopes that it would clinch a Nixon victory in November. The governor was a staunch Democrat and a Kennedy supporter. Before November, in a meeting with Kennedy at the Waldorf Astoria in New York, Patterson confided to the presidential hopeful what the CIA agent had told him about secret plans to invade Cuba. Patterson said he believed an invasion was imminent and, if successful, would be used to defeat Kennedy at the polls in November. [3]

There were others who believed Vice President Richard Nixon wanted dramatic action taken against Castro before the election, but Eisenhower was not going to let that happen. The President had not approved any plan to invade Cuba and had no intention of doing so. He had given his approval for a secret program to train and equip anti-Castro Cuban refugees, but there had been no decisions as to how the forces would be used, if at all. [4] Kennedy did not reveal to the governor that CIA Director Allen Dulles had already briefed him in July at Hyannis Port about training Cuban exiles for operations against the Castro government. [5]

Governor Patterson's fears proved unfounded when Kennedy narrowly defeated his Republican opponent in the November election. Meanwhile, General Doster and his staff had begun

Arkansas Governor Orval Faubus, Brigadier General Reid Doster, and
Brigadier General Frank Bailey, chief of staff of the Arkansas Air
National Guard (AANG photo).

planning in secret for the Air Guard's participation in the CIA
project. Once the plan became final Doster pulled together a group
of 80 volunteers from among present and former Air Guard members. Most of the volunteers were from Alabama, but a few came
from Arkansas and elsewhere. After the Cuban invasion failed Orval
E. Faubus, who served three terms (1955-1967) as the Arkansas
governor, appeared to have second thoughts about his state's involvement in the operation.

In March 1963 the wire services reported an admission by
Governor Faubus that the CIA had secretly recruited some Arkansas guardsmen on "a soldier of fortune basis" from the 184th
Tactical Reconnaissance Squadron at Fort Smith. The governor
claimed that some Arkansans had flown combat missions and that

an Arkansas Guard plane on loan to the CIA had been shot down.[6] United Press International quoted Brigadier General Frank Bailey, chief of staff of the Arkansas Air National Guard, as saying: "He (Faubus) doesn't know what he's talking about. The Air Guard did not have any planes involved." The general was quick to add that the governor might be privy to information the Guard did not have.[7]

According to the UPI report, Governor Faubus lashed out at the federal government for "secretly recruiting Arkansas National Guard pilots for the 1961 Cuban invasion" and for the way the government handled the operation:

> This whole thing is a disgrace in American history. They tried to recruit some men in the north and couldn't do it, so they came down to the South where they still have some patriotism and got some volunteers among the National Guard.[8]

THE FINAL WEEKS of 1960 were busy ones for General Doster's wing headquarters. The wing was already on a fast track—having transitioned into Republic RF-84F jets in the spring of 1958—but the CIA mission took priority and demanded their immediate attention. Doster called his key staff together and had them begin planning for the secret mission in Guatemala. Two senior staffers, Lieutenant Colonel Joseph L. Shannon (commander of the Alabama Guard's 106th Bombardment Squadron) and Major Riley Shamburger (squadron operations officer), went to CIA headquarters in Washington for six weeks to provide technical guidance and to help out with command post operations.[9]

Shannon and Shamburger were two of Doster's most experienced officers. At 39 years of age, Shannon was a soft-spoken professional who had flown fighters throughout the Mediterranean theater during WWII and was cool under fire. He flew the Lockheed

Above: Joe Shannon, an AANG captain in 1947, climbs into the cockpit of an Air Guard B-26 bomber (courtesy of Joe Shannon).

Left: Major Riley Shamburger, killed in action at the Bay of Pigs (Southern Museum of Flight photo).

P-38 Lightning in the war and was the first Allied pilot to land safely in Italy after that invasion. Shannon's fellow guardsmen called him "Shaky Joe" because he was so unflappable.

Shamburger, also a WWII veteran, was a couple of years younger than his squadron commander, a larger man, more boisterous and carefree. Called "Hambone" by some of his friends, Shamburger had a hair-trigger temper, but was described as "dynamic, a man's man, and a leader" who was well-liked and respected in the Alabama Guard.[10]

At CIA headquarters Allen Dulles and his people were looking forward to moving to a new facility at Langley, Virginia, early in 1961, but the Agency's clandestine operations in places like Laos and Cuba were the center of attention in the fall of 1960. Of special interest to the Alabama guardsmen were operations of the Cuban Task Force that was set up early in 1960 in response to President Eisenhower's "request for an ambitious covert program to over-throw the Castro government." Under the overall direction of Richard Bissell, the CIA's chief of clandestine services, the task force was headed by Jake Esterline, a specialist in covert operations who helped oust the communist regime of Jacobo Arbenz in Guatemala in 1954.[11] In August 1960, the Marines detailed Colonel Jack Hawkins, a crack combat officer with experience in amphibious landings, to the CIA for the planned paramilitary assault against Cuba. Stanley W. Beerli, a razor-thin, balding USAF colonel on detached duty with the CIA, was in charge of air support for the invasion.[12]

From their discussions in Washington the Alabama guardsmen learned that the CIA had been training Cuban guerrillas in the Canal Zone and in the United States, primarily on Useppa Island off Florida's southwest coast, since the spring of 1960. The Agency needed a larger, more realistic training base and an airfield from which air transports flown by Cuban exiles and contract pilots could resupply resistance fighters in the Sierra Maestra and Escambray mountain ranges in Cuba. The Guatemalan government agreed to a CIA proposal to build a secret airfield at Retalhuleu in the Sierra Madre Mountains, and in early July the training program for Cuban exiles was moved from Useppa Island to bases in Guatemala. The Sierra Madre range was a realistic training ground for the airdrop missions over the rugged mountains in Cuba. The new facilities at Retalhuleu also supported training for larger actions against the Castro regime.[13]

The CIA used several training areas in Guatemala. The primary ones were located near Retalhuleu at Helvetia and La Sviza, two vast coffee plantations in the Sierra Madre Mountains owned by Roberto Alejos, the brother of the Guatemalan ambassador to the United States, Carlos Alejos. The ambassador obtained approval from President Ydigoras Fuentes for the CIA to arm and train Cuban anti-Castro forces on Guatemalan soil, and arranged for the use of his brother's plantations as training bases. Roberto Alejos was compensated for the use of his plantations, and got a new airfield nearby as a bonus. The CIA and the Guatemalans mutually benefited from the arrangement, although questions would arise afterward whether a "worse training site" could have been chosen. A lack of facilities, torrential rains, volcanic soil, and thousands of inquisitive plantation workers were just a few of the problems that plagued CIA planning for the invasion. In terms of security, the base was in plain view of a busy railway and a road that was jammed with trucks carrying coffee beans and workers from nearby plantations.[14]

Even before construction started on the Retalhuleu airfield, the Castro government accused Guatemala of serving "as a bridgehead for an invasion of our country." By the fall of 1960 the rumors were rampant that Cuban exiles were training at Retalhuleu for an invasion of Cuba. President Fuentes went on television to admit the existence of the base, but this only added fuel to the rumor mill.

Around the same time the thinking at CIA headquarters began shifting from "infiltrating teams to wage guerrilla warfare to an amphibious operation involving at least 1,500 men who would seize and defend an area by sea and air assault and establish a base for further operations."[15]

It was painfully obvious by the fall of 1960 that Castro was not likely to be defeated by the resistance movement alone. The infiltration of guerrillas and their resupply from the air was proving more difficult than CIA planners had thought. A report described the first drop of weapons and supplies to the Cuban resistance in September 1960:

> The air crew tries to drop an arms pack for a hundred men to an agent waiting on the ground. They miss the drop zone by seven miles and land the weapons on top of a dam where they are picked up by Castro's forces. The agent is caught and shot. The plane gets lost on the way to Guatemala and lands in Mexico, where it is impounded.[16]

It did not take a military strategist to see that the base at Retalhuleu was not a suitable jumping-off point for an invasion of Cuba. The base was a mountain fortress built on a plateau overlooking the Pacific and was not strategically located for an amphibious assault on Cuba. The ships could not embark from Retalhuleu without going through the Panama Canal, and the base was beyond the range of fully armed B-26s. The CIA had begun searching for a more suitable base, one that was in the combat radius of fully loaded B-26s and supporting aircraft, from which to launch the invasion once training was completed in Guatemala. A remote airstrip at Puerto Cabezas on the northeastern coast of Nicaragua was the only operating location available, and it barely met the range requirements. On December 8, the CIA task force got approval to negotiate for the use of Puerto Cabezas as a staging base for the Cuban invasion.[17]

Subsequently, Colonel Beerli called on an old friend of the Alabama Guard to survey the base at Puerto Cabezas and to help negotiate with Nicaragua strong man Anastasio Somoza for its use. Lieutenant Colonel Harry C. "Heinie" Aderholt, who was born and raised in Birmingham, had been with the CIA since the Korean War and now commanded clandestine air operations out of Okinawa and Thailand. Heinie Aderholt knew most of the Alabama Guard pilots. His brother Warren, an Air Force fighter jock, had served with the Alabama Guard after returning from WWII. He was delighted to hear that Reid Doster and the guardsmen were an integral part of the Cuban operation.[18]

When the resupply missions got off to a bad start in September the task force asked for Aderholt's help in training the Cuban transport pilots at Retalhuleu. An expert in covert air operations, Aderholt had dropped agents behind the lines during the Korean War and had set up the CIA's first air training school at Williamsburg, Virginia. He sent the task force a couple of his best pilots to help train the Cubans at Retalhuleu to fly C-46 Commando and C-54 Skymaster transports in clandestine operations. On a hurried trip back to Washington, Aderholt went with officials from the Central American Division to negotiate with Nicaragua's president Anastasio Somoza for permission to stage the Cuban invasion out of Puerto Cabezas.[19]

The team met secretly with the Nicaraguan president at 2 A.M. on a sultry tropic night. After getting Somoza's permission to use Puerto Cabezas, Aderholt flew with Somoza's son, Anastasio Jr., in a C-47 to inspect the field, which was an old World War II strip on the way to Panama with swamps all around it. While there he made a sketch of the field and its 5,000-foot cinder runway for the CIA to use in preparing for the invasion. Aderholt never forgot President

Somoza's parting words to the CIA team. "I'm willing to support you," he said, speaking of plans to overthrow Fidel Castro, "but be sure you get rid of that son of a bitch, or you are going to live with him the rest of your life."[20]

BACK IN BIRMINGHAM, General Doster's recruiting efforts picked up around the Christmas Holidays. After briefing President-elect Kennedy at Palm Beach, Florida, on November 18 and getting high-level authorization on December 8 to proceed with its plans, the CIA task force began a seven-week training program at a base camp near Retalhuleu for approximately 600 Cuban exiles. While the CIA continued to train some guerrilla forces in Guatemala, the new program was much larger and entailed conventional training for an amphibious and airborne assault.[21] Soon thereafter, the CIA gave Doster the word to press on with efforts to recruit a force of approximately eighty Air Guard volunteers.

All the CIA asked of General Doster was that he recruit qualified volunteers to serve as advisers to the Cuban B-26 pilots at Retalhuleu, to fly some transport missions, and to arm and maintain the planes. The agency neither needed nor wanted the Air Guard general to deploy to Retalhuleu with the Alabama volunteers. The agency stationed one of its officers (known only by a pseudonym, Gar) at the base as commander of air operations. Another CIA officer was assigned as his deputy. The presence of an Air Guard general at the base could only confuse the chain of command and get in the way of operations. Doster insisted on being with "his boys," however, so he took temporary leave from the Guard. The CIA, needing his support and cooperation, took him along as part of a package deal. One advantage of having Doster there was that he got along famously with the Cuban pilots, who enjoyed being around the general and respected him.[22]

When Joe Shannon and Riley Shamburger went to CIA headquarters in early January 1961, they helped Colonel Beerli's people finalize B-26 requirements. Beerli's deputy for air operations, Colonel George Gaines, was in charge of putting the B-26 project together. The 16 refurbished B-26s along with additional C-46 and C-54 transports would be at Retalhuleu waiting for the guardsmen when they got there. Some 40 former commercial and military pilots were selected from among Cuban exiles in Miami to undergo training at Retalhuleu. General Doster's volunteers were charged with getting the B-26s and their Cuban pilots ready for the invasion. Doster recruited a few civilian pilots as backup to the CIA regulars flying the C-46 and C-54 transports. He also needed crew chiefs, armament specialists, mechanics, and firemen. Most of these specialties were filled by the Alabama Guard, but some came from Arkansas and Georgia.[23]

General Doster called the guardsmen into his headquarters, individually and in groups, and gruffly warned them about the secrecy surrounding their mission. The ones who volunteered for the mission were instructed not to tell their families or anyone else where they were going. They made up "believable" cover stories to hide their identity and to mislead interrogators in the event they were captured. Doster had the entire wing fired up about the mission, but not everyone could go. Not only were there not enough slots in Guatemala for all of the guardsmen, but there were other exigencies to consider. Many of the guardsmen were married and had families. Most had civilian jobs or their own businesses. Joe Shannon said he had to give the matter a lot of thought before telling Doster in late December that he would go. While he and Riley Shamburger were in Washington, the other guardsmen began shipping out to Retalhuleu in January.[24]

Volunteers for the CIA mission made a dent in the workforce at Hayes Aircraft Corporation sitting across the field from the Air Guard wing. Shamburger, Billy "Dodo" Goodwin, Dalton "Stud"

Livingston, George Nelms and Thomas Ray were test pilots with Hayes which did repair and maintenance work for the Air Force. Leo Francis Baker and Wade Carroll Gray were flight engineers with the corporation. Baker also operated two pizza parlors in Birmingham. Another Air Guard pilot, James W. "Jaws" Harrison, Jr., a veteran of World War II and the Korean War, was employed by Hayes as an inspector. He and some of the other pilots thought they would be flying combat missions against Cuba, not finding out until after arriving in Guatemala that they would be training Cubans to fly.[25]

Albert C. "Buck" Persons was a civilian pilot who jumped at the chance to join the group of Air Guard volunteers and who later wrote a book about the experience. A multifaceted individual who was drawn to adventure throughout his life, Buck Persons as a young man had joined the Royal Canadian Air Force in 1939 when World War II started. After the Bay of Pigs he became managing editor of a weekly newspaper, the *Birmingham Examiner*. He had not joined the Alabama Guard, but had friends in Doster's wing and, being somewhat bored with his job flying a DC-3 for a Birmingham construction firm, was a natural choice for the CIA mission in Guatemala. Just after New Year's Day, Persons knew something was up when he arrived at the hangar around noon to find a message that Riley Shamburger had been trying all morning to reach him.[26]

Persons tracked his friend down at the Hayes Aircraft hangars. Shamburger, who was in a rush because he and Shannon were getting ready to leave for Washington, explained that General Doster was recruiting pilots for a hush-hush mission in Guatemala and sent Persons over to the wing headquarters to see him. After he and a group of other pilots were briefed on the mission Persons signed up. Doster leaned heavily on the men not to reveal to anyone where they were going or what they would be doing, warning in a

booming voice that "their ass was grass" if they did. Although
Doster did not mention Fidel Castro or Cuba, Persons said that it
was obvious to everyone what their mission would be and the stories
were all over the newspapers anyway.[27]

Armament and maintenance personnel were among the first
guardsmen to leave Birmingham on the secret mission. The list
included Captain William P. Baker and two top noncoms, John O.
Spinks and Louis H. Hudson. Spinks was one of two men volun-
teering for the mission who could mix napalm. He also was one of
the elders in the Alabama Air National Guard, having joined up in
1937 while working in a steel mill. In 1940 Spinks and other
members of the Birmingham-based unit were called up and served
with the Thirteenth Air Force in the South Pacific. When the war
ended, he returned home and accepted a full-time position with the
Air Guard. As always, Spinks was ready to go wherever he was
needed when General Doster called him and the other two guardsmen into his office and warned, "Breathe one word of what I am
going to tell you and I'll have your ass." The general then grinned
broadly and asked, "How would you guys like to kick Castro's
butt?"[28]

Reid Doster was a noncom's general. Most of them respected
Doster, and they liked his style. Bobby A. Whitley, who was in
communications and radio repair at Puerto Cabezas, said Doster
was "smart" and "a good leader," but was overbearing at times. "If
he wasn't so overbearing he could have got men to follow him
anywhere in the world," Whitley said. "But it was his way or no way.
His opinion was the only one that counted. If he treated his men
right they would have done anything in the world for him."[29]

Roy H. Wilson, another sergeant who left for Guatemala after
Spinks and Hudson, thought "Papa" Doster could do no wrong.
He described Doster as "a hell of a commander, a hell of a general."
He related an incident involving a new 1956 Ford convertible he

Alabama air guardsmen during "Happy Hour" at Airport Inn in
Birmingham before going to Guatemala. (L to R) Jim Terry, Riley
Shamburger, Charles Crow, Clarence Saterwhite (owner), Billy Joe
Goodwin, Dave Hatter, and Bobby Whitley. (courtesy of Bobby
Whitley)

bought soon after joining the Guard. "Man, I was proud of that
car!" Wilson recalled. One morning he unwittingly parked the Ford
in a space that a major had reserved for his personal use. "The son
of a bitch ran into the side of my convertible and left a note for me
to never park there again," Wilson said. "I went to the major's office
and told him if he didn't fix my car, I was going to whip the major's
ass." The major went to General Doster, who told the officer he was
not authorized a private parking space and assured him that Roy
Wilson was a man of his word. The major paid for having the
convertible repaired.[30]

Wilson confirmed what others said about there being no need
for the general at Retalhuleu or Puerto Cabezas, however. "I can't

The last B-26 retired from the Alabama Air National Guard in November 1957 (Don Crocker Collection, Southern Museum of Flight).

recall seeing him (Doster) do one damn thing," Wilson told an interviewer. Once when the general put Wilson and another non-com to work uncrating guns, a CIA supervisor came by and asked what they were doing. When the men explained that "Papa" had told them to take the guns out of the crates, the CIA honcho yelled at Doster and asked what he was doing giving the men orders. "They were sitting on their butts doing nothing and I thought I would put them to work," Doster replied. The general was reminded that the men worked for the CIA, not him. "We went back to sitting on our butts," Wilson said.[31]

Before going to Guatemala, Roy Wilson supplemented his Alabama Guard pay by moonlighting as a bartender at the Airport Inn, a popular hangout for the air guardsmen and the Hayes pilots.

Wilson said he had seen "the sun rise there lots of times." The Air Guard members gathered at the inn the night before leaving Birmingham to go on the Cuban mission and partied there when they came back.[32] Sometimes reporters came to the Airport Inn looking for a good story. The Birmingham warriors didn't stand on protocol, and anyone could forget that "loose lips sink ships" when the beer was flowing and their hair was down.

David Langford with *The Birmingham News* was one of the reporters who broke the news in the spring of 1961 about the Alabama Guard's connection to the Bay of Pigs invasion. Twenty-five years later Langford looked back on Alabama's support for the Cuban invasion in a news feature he wrote for the Associated Press. Portraying them as "mostly laid-back, beer-drinking sons of Dixie" led by "a bullish general" who called them "his little airmen" and was "eager to kick Castro's tail," Langford recalled the electricity that was in the air when the guardsmen began leaving for Guatemala in late 1960. "The rumor mill was working overtime at the Airport Inn, the beer and barbecue joint near the Birmingham airport where Hayes technicians and Air Guardsmen usually ended their flights," Langford wrote. Regulars at the bar were conspicuously absent, and people were asking questions. "Most figured Papa (Doster) was up to something," he stated. "Soon there was talk of an operation 'down south.'"[33]

2

Training in Guatemala

EIGHT HUNDRED MILES to the south the rumors buzzing around Birmingham's municipal airport were nothing compared to those sweeping through "Little Havana" in Miami. The exile community in Miami had become a hotbed of political intrigue since Fidel Castro's rise to power, with 100-plus Cuban political factions at work in Florida and 1,000 anti-Castro emigres arriving each week. There was no keeping quiet the fact in early 1961 that hundreds of recruits were shipping out for military training in Guatemala. Reports on the numbers of volunteers leaving Miami were inflated for the most part, but the news media's overall coverage of the buildup was right on target.

The Miami newspapers and the national media reported freely that a huge buildup was underway in Central America to overthrow the Castro regime. *U.S. News & World Report* informed the world in March 1961 that preparations for an invasion of Cuba were in the final stages. The story claimed that trucks carrying 243 Cuban volunteers recently left Miami on the first leg of a journey to training camps in the Caribbean area, while 500 others stood by awaiting transport. "Still others were going to the recruiting offices of the Democratic Revolutionary Front here to sign up," the report stated.[1] Castro did not need the hundreds of spies who were planted within the exile community to know what was going on.

The truth was that only a few C-54 flights carrying recruits arrived at Retalhuleu monthly. There were approximately 50 recruits on each flight. Upon unloading at Retalhuleu they were trucked up the mountains into the clouds to an isolated training camp known as Base Trax. The base was on the Helvetia coffee plantation, five thousand rugged acres sprawling below the still-active Santiaguita volcano. The nucleus of a combat brigade had been formed in November at Base Trax to prepare for the buildup, which could not begin in earnest until after the U.S. Presidential inaugural in January. The unit was named Brigade 2506, in honor of Carlos Rafael Santana (2506 was Santana's serial number), who was the first member of the group to die in a training accident. The brigade, which started with 400 troops, never grew to more than 1,500 men while preparing for the assault on Cuba.[2]

Brigade 2506 emblem.

The undersized brigade was composed of six light infantry battalions, a heavy weapons battalion, an armored truck battalion, and a tank company. Initial plans called for a buildup to as many as 5,000 men after the brigade landed in Cuba. The plans anticipated that the liberation force would gain additional recruits from the Cuban populace, relying on a general uprising against the Castro government to provide the additional manpower. This overreliance on a Cuban uprising, which was not supported by intelligence reports coming from the island, revealed a basic flaw in the CIA's planning for the invasion.[3]

Near the end of January 1961, about the time President Kennedy received his first formal briefing on the Cuban operation, a JCS study group under Army Brigadier General David W. Gray reviewed the CIA plan and gave it only a 30 percent chance of succeeding. The group concluded that the invading force might last up to four days if it had "complete surprise and complete air supremacy." The invasion had to spark popular uprisings to have any hope of overthrowing the Castro government. Meanwhile, the CIA was reminded of how tenuous its plans were when two hundred Cuban exiles revolted at the training camp in Guatemala. To quell the revolt the CIA removed twelve troublemakers and held them in improvised jungle prisons until the invasion was over.[4]

THE ALABAMA GUARD's three-man team of Baker, Hudson, and Spinks arrived at Retalhuleu before the swarm of new Cuban recruits began reporting to the training camps in Guatemala. When they left Birmingham the team, wearing civilian clothes with the labels removed, had taken a commercial flight to Houston, Texas, then onto Guatemala City. They were met by U.S. Embassy personnel who arranged for their travel to Retalhuleu. Baker described Retalhuleu as "a first-class bad base . . . a civilian airfield with an air terminal but everything in bad shape."[5]

B-26 bomber with Cuban markings at Puerto Cabezas, Nicaragua, before the Bay of Pigs Invasion (courtesy of Colonel Mike Haas, USAF Ret.).

The CIA's operations at Retalhuleu were in their infancy when Baker's small team arrived. Baker recalled that he and the two senior sergeants with him "were poorly supported in every way." They were welcomed to the base by a small USAF contingent led by Air Force Colonel Billy Campbell and a half-dozen men from the Georgia Air National Guard. According to Lou Hudson, the Georgia Guard got involved with the CIA project first and recommended that the CIA contact General Doster because the Birmingham wing was the last Guard unit to fly the B-26s. Spinks said they put up tents on the flightline at Retalhuleu to train the Cubans. "We would set up a machine gun in a tent and teach the Cubans to take it apart and put it back together again," Spinks said.[6]

Working with the CIA—which was a loose operation compared to what the military men were accustomed to—was a new experience for the three Alabama guardsmen. The situation was complicated by the fact that the host country, although no longer in the throes of revolution, was still politically unstable. At one point some of the B-26s were flown to the Guatemalan capital to help the Fuentes government defend itself against a purported coup attempt. Lou Hudson and some other guardsmen went with the B-26s to arm the bombers and to keep them flying. They were there about a week. "There was a lot of military activity . . . troops marching around everywhere," Hudson recalled. "We were glad to get back to our base."[7]

Guatemalan soldiers converged on Retalhuleu and set up camp, ostensibly to guard the base against communist guerrillas. Captain Baker had a run-in with Colonel Campbell because he wanted to establish a defense perimeter on base during the political unrest. Campbell ordered the men not to take up arms to defend themselves. When Baker objected, the colonel relieved him and sent him back to Eglin AFB, Florida, where the CIA secretly operated an auxiliary field nearby. From Eglin, Baker went back to Birmingham and was relieved by General Doster. Baker said he briefed Doster on everything that was going on in Guatemala, and told the general that he thought it was an impossible situation. Doster did not believe him, Baker said. When asked what he thought of Doster, Baker said that he was "sort of a smart aleck, but a good leader."[8]

Hudson and Spinks along with other armament specialists and mechanics later went to Eglin from Guatemala for a few weeks to work on the B-26s and their armament, but were back at Puerto Cabezas in time to support the invasion. The two senior noncoms were part of the Alabama commitment from start to finish. Among other crewmen (including flight engineers) going on the secret mission were Leo Baker, Warren Brown, Johnny Burton, Donald Chandler, Willie Colvert, Donald Crocker, Joseph Fancher, William Fultz, Tom Gillespie, James Glenn, Melvin Harvey, Joel Kilgore, Harold Martin, Jack Mohon, Will Pullen, Fred Raley, Carl

Bobby Whitley, left, and Bill Gray, as they appeared in their Tarrant HS Class of 1950 yearbook photos (courtesy of Bobby Whitley).

Sudano, Robert Stanley, Benny Strawn, Bobby Whitley, and Charles Yates. A two-man fire department made up of Bill Gray and Glenn Monaghan joined their fellow guardsmen at Puerto Cabezas. Some of the B-26 crews went to Retalhuleu and some to Puerto Cabezas, according to where they were needed. Hudson found it interesting that some of the B-26s they worked on at Eglin left for Vietnam instead of taking part in the Cuban invasion.[9]

While they were back at Eglin, the CIA questioned them about how things were going in Guatemala. Hudson echoed Captain Baker's complaint that "operations were not too smooth" and that "no one was really in charge." He recommended they send General Doster to Guatemala. "He was a take-charge guy. He had his faults but he was the best guy in the world," Hudson said of Doster. "He ran the show. He told you what to do and you did it." Unlike what others have said, Hudson had the impression that "General Doster

Cuban exile paratroopers making practice jumps over Retalhuleu air base in Guatemala (courtesy of Colonel Mike Haas, USAF Ret.).

was in charge in Nicaragua" when the Cuban invasion was launched.[10]

Being with the operation "for the long haul" gave Spinks and Hudson a different perspective on the Cuban exiles from that of Captain Baker. During the relatively brief period Baker was in Guatemala he said that he "was embarrassed about what was going on there." "The Cubans were unable to arm and maintain the aircraft and didn't seem to want to learn," he asserted. "It was apparent they couldn't handle the operation and I'm not sure we could have ever brought in enough people to train them to do so."[11]

John Spinks, however, stated that training the Cubans was like most training, "good and bad." Fortunately there was a Cuban, Ramon Sanchez, who spoke fluent English and helped greatly in training. "The Cubans were friendly and appreciated us being there," Spinks said. James Glenn, an aircraft electrician who worked on the B-26s at Puerto Cabezas also contradicted the assertion that the Cuban mechanics could not maintain their aircraft. Glenn recalled the Cuban mechanics sending him away when he went over to work on one of their B-26s. "They wanted to maintain their own aircraft," Glenn said. "They had pride in doing it themselves."[12]

Lou Hudson echoed their sentiments. According to Hudson, the only reason Alabama guardsmen had to take part in arming and maintaining the B-26s was because there were not enough Cubans to do the job. Hudson found the Cubans to be "very competent" and "really, really good guys." "We were around the Cubans for some time and made friends with them," he said. "We had a mission with a purpose. It was an experience you couldn't have anywhere else, a one-of-a-kind operation."[13]

IN JANUARY A MUCH LARGER group of Alabama volunteers, including B-26 and C-54 pilots, left Birmingham on their way to Guatemala. Among these pilots were Eldon Cross, Billy Joe Goodwin, James Harrison, Ulay Littleton, Dalton "Stud" Livingston, George

(L to R) Major Billy Joe Goodwin, Brigadier General Reid Doster, and two unidentified Cuban pilots wearing the uniform of the day at the secret CIA base at Retalhuleu, Guatemala (courtesy of Colonel Mike Haas, USAF Ret.).

Nelms, Albert Persons, Thomas Ray, and Charles Weldon. Before they departed, Colonel Beerli and members of his staff briefed them at the wing headquarters in Birmingham, going over their cover stories and giving them instructions on travel arrangements. Albert Persons recalled that two men who asked too many questions at the briefing were dismissed from the group. The remaining volunteers, as instructed, purchased airline tickets separately or in pairs for flights to Miami where they had reservations at the McAlister Hotel.

Despite precautions that were taken to keep the trip from looking like a troop movement, nearly all of the men ended up on the same flight to Miami anyway, according to Persons, because everyone waited until the last minute to leave their families. They pulled up to the McAlister Hotel in a string of taxis and trooped into the lobby at the same time, all of them "looking self-conscious and conspiratorial." Persons said they were reminded of this faux pas in no uncertain terms in the days ahead. "In those days in Miami, a low profile was the uniform of the day," he said. The men spent several days in Miami, where they were given fake identification papers and further instructions.[14]

From Miami the B-26 crews and the C-54 crews departed in separate groups for Retalhuleu. The bomber crews were flown to Retalhuleu from an abandoned Navy airfield at Opa-Locka, in suburban Miami.[15] Sixteen refurbished B-26s and forty Cuban pilots were there waiting when the guardsmen arrived. Some of the exile pilots, like Captain Edward B. Ferrer, had been flying for the CIA in Guatemala before the completion of Retalhuleu (called Rayo for short) in September. A Cubana Airlines pilot who hijacked his own flight at gunpoint in July 1960 to reach freedom in the United States, Ferrer had been in contact with the CIA before leaving Havana. He and other exile pilots began flying missions in support of the resistance movement in Cuba within weeks of touching down in Miami.[16]

Ferrer observed that more and more Americans were arriving daily in January 1961. The Alabama guardsmen had been fore-warned to expect primitive living conditions at Retalhuleu, but the base's facilities were no worse than those on the hundreds of airfields carved out of the jungle in the Pacific during WWII or in Korea in the summer of 1950. Lou Hudson described the living conditions as "terrible," but noted that the facilities at Retalhuleu were better than those at Puerto Cabezas. At Retalhuleu the Americans were in one barracks, and the 100 or so Cubans in the flying program were in other barracks. When they moved to Puerto Cabezas they lived in tents where snakes and scorpions were unwanted houseguests, used outdoor privies and drainage ditches for urinals, and there was never enough water for showers. "There was a mudhole out back of the tents, and we all wondered if that's where the water came from," Hudson said with a shrug.[17]

There were the occasional mishaps that accompany a military operation in the field. Roy Wilson accidentally shot himself in the hand while checking the safety on a Colt .45. James Glenn said Wilson wanted to know who had "loaded that damn gun." "Of course it wasn't funny then but it was later," Glenn said. Wilson was flown back to Birmingham for medical treatment. While there his "cover story" was that he had stuck a nail through his hand. During a recent interview Bob Whitley said he still kidded Wilson about "the .45 penny nail."[18]

Many of the guardsmen who were at Retalhuleu or Puerto Cabezas for an extended period got at least one opportunity to fly back to Birmingham to see their families. Joe Shannon said he made one or two trips back to Miami, and one to Birmingham. According to Riley Shamburger's wife, her husband flew into Birmingham with General Doster about every other week. On one return visit, Riley told his wife how the boys in Central America had rigged up a beer joint in a tent and named it after their favorite Birmingham hangout, the Airport Inn. Thomas Ray, Leo Baker, and Wade Gray also made brief visits home. None of the men told their wives where they had been or what they were doing, but the wives were able to piece things together from reading the newspapers.[19]

James Glenn, an aircraft electrician with the Alabama Guard, was one of the crewmen who worked with the CIA at Eglin and at Puerto Cabezas, but did not go to Guatemala. Glenn recalled that the mess hall at Puerto Cabezas was in a tent and the food was edible. "We sometimes had Cuban food like black beans and rice," he said.[20] Among the cooks at Puerto Cabezas were William D. "Bill" Bainbridge, Jack Bates, Carroll Sullivan, and Arvin Moore.

Bainbridge recalled that the cooks went to Nicaragua together in a C-54, flying at night and on the deck to avoid detection by radar. Only a few people ate at the mess hall when the cooks first arrived, but they started feeding several hundred tired and hungry troops just before the invasion.[21]

Bainbridge said that Anastasio Somoza, the Nicaraguan strong man, visited the field on one occasion and ate lunch at the mess hall. He described the event:

> There were three men on either side of Somoza in civilian clothes, and six to eight military guys with guns surrounding him. I asked one who spoke English why they didn't let us know they were coming so we could have prepared a special meal. He said, 'We always travel unannounced. That's how he stays alive.'[22]

When they were off duty the guardsmen mostly drank beer, according to Bobby Whitley, but occasionally they played touch football for recreation. Once when the troops loaded into a truck and went to a nearby river to swim, they had to compete with crocodiles sunning on the opposite bank. The troops left and did not go back. Glenn said they had a bar in a tent with a parachute spread out overhead. "We called it the Airport Inn, what else," Glenn said, adding thoughtfully, "We had some good times there." Bainbridge recalled that the mess hall hours were flexible. "We would have 'Happy Hour' at the Airport Inn around 5 p.m. and then wander on down to the mess tent when we got ready to eat," he said. When asked what kind of beer they drank, he said, "Any kind they flew in."[23]

There were the usual "midnight requisitions" that are legend in military life. Once when the ice cooler where the guardsmen stored their beer broke down, a civilian in work clothes came and hauled the cooler "beer and all" away on a forklift. The phony repairman claimed he had been sent to pick up the ice cooler and take it back to the shop to fix it. When the repairman did not return, the guardsmen went looking for him. All they found was the empty cooler. They learned later that their culprit was an Army special forces adviser who had figured out a clever way to "requisition" their beer.[24]

At Retalhuleu the club was located in a small wooden building, which had been constructed by Guatemalan laborers before the Alabama guardsmen arrived. The club created dissension when first built because it was off limits to Cubans unless they were invited inside by an American. The Cuban pilots and crews understood why they were denied access to other buildings such as the command post and armory, but resented having the club closed to them. The restriction was later removed, but Captain Ferrer, in his book *Operation Puma*, wrote that a great deal of bitterness resulted from the club incident and it would take a long time for a return to friendly relations between the Cubans and their advisers. "Fortunately, the animosity between the two groups dissolved with time and feelings of true brotherhood grew in its place," Ferrer wrote.[25]

The Cuban pilots suspected that their American advisers were military pilots, but were not certain because they all wore casual civilian clothing and were known by their *noms de guerre*. The men in both groups were professionals in pursuit of a common cause and, despite misunderstandings like the club incident, succeeded in overcoming their cultural and language differences. Captain Ferrer recalled the difficulties the Cuban pilots had with the Southern accents and idiomatic expressions of their Alabama advisers. He recounted an amusing incident that would never have happened had he and the other Cuban pilots known that Reid Doster was a general in the Alabama Air National Guard.[26]

When Doster first got to Retalhuleu the Cubans had no idea who he was. No one had told them that the man wearing tennis shoes whose large frame was bulging out of a T-shirt and shorts was a general officer. While on an orientation flight with Joaquin Varela, a B-26 squadron commander, Doster was instructed to keep his hands off the controls. In his usual fatherly tone, the general smiled and said, "Okay, sonny." When they were back on the ground the angry pilot chewed Doster out for calling a former Cuban naval officer "sonny." With an amused look Doster replied, "Okay, sonny," and walked away. Years later at a reunion in Miami, Varela apologized for the incident and asked if Doster remembered it. "Sure do, sonny," Doster said.[27]

Except for the clandestine aspects of the mission, the austere conditions and time constraints, the Air Guard's task at Retalhuleu was not that different from numerous other third-world military training programs carried out by U.S. servicemen around the world. As a matter of fact, the CIA had another secret B-26 operation known as "Mill Pond" underway in Thailand at the same time. Lieutenant Colonel Heinie Aderholt, who helped negotiate with Nicarauguan President Somoza for the CIA's use of Puerto Cabeza, had assembled a dozen or more B-26s at Takhli, Thailand, for strikes against communist strongholds in Laos. The strikes in Laos were to have been launched the morning after the Cuban invasion, but were called off by President Kennedy when things started going badly at the Bay of Pigs.[28]

A major distinction between the two bomber operations was that USAF pilots were detailed to the CIA for the strikes in Laos, while Cuban exile pilots were preparing to fly the combat missions from Puerto Cabezas. Neither group of pilots had flown bombers in wartime and had to be trained in combat tactics—bombing, strafing, and maneuvering to avoid enemy fire. While none of the Cuban pilots had been in air combat, most were experienced pilots and some had military backgrounds. Several of the pilots were flying transport and airdrop missions before the Alabama guardsmen

arrived. The ones who had been selected to fly the B-26s in support
of the invasion spent valuable time at Retalhuleu honing their
combat skills.

James Harrison said that he and three other instructors (Littleton,
Livingston, and Goodwin) taught the Cuban pilots to fly B-26s in
close formation. The pilots learned much-needed aerial gunnery
skills. There was no gunnery range available, so the Cuban pilots
made effective use of a remote lake about twenty-five miles inland
from Retalhuleu for target practice. They constructed crude rafts—
using bamboo poles, boards, and 50-gallon drums lashed together
with wire—and dropped them onto the lake from C-46 and C-54
transports. The makeshift targets were used almost daily for gunnery and rocket practice. Bob Whitley recalled Studs Livingston
saying they sometimes went out over the ocean and strafed sharks.
The B-26 pilots were ready to go into combat by the time they left
Retalhuleu. Lou Hudson said they "had a lot more training before
going into combat than some of our guys in World War II."[29]

Although of WWII-vintage the B-26 was an ideal aircraft for
operations in undeveloped areas of the world. When fully armed the
bomber carried a deadly mix of ordnance, including machine guns,
rockets, iron bombs or napalm. The B-26 had no air-to-air capability, however, and was an easy target for enemy fighters. A recent
reminder of the bomber's vulnerability had occurred during a CIA-
supported military insurrection in 1958 when an Indonesian Air
Force P-51 shot down a B-26 piloted by an American mercenary.
The Alabama Air Guard pilots knew they had to destroy Castro's air
force during the hours preceding the invasion, or all was lost.[30]

Neither the guardsmen nor the Cuban aircrews were overly
concerned about the air-to-air threat because they knew that plans
called for attaining complete control of the air before launching the
invasion. Lieutenant Colonel Shannon and Major Shamburger had
worked with Colonel Beerli's staff at CIA headquarters on plans for

employing the B-26s during the invasion. The B-26s were to carry out heavy and sustained pre-invasion strikes against Cuban airfields to destroy all of Castro's military planes while still on the ground. Beerli and his staff were professional airmen and knew their jobs. Another Air Force officer, General Charles P. Cabell, was the principal deputy under Allen Dulles. The Alabama guardsmen saw no reason why planning should go awry. James Glenn recalled Riley Shamburger coming by before the first air strikes and declaring: "There is no way this is going to fail." "We all thought we were going to win," Glenn said.[31]

As MILITARY MEN the guardsmen were accustomed to being given a mission to do, but not being told how to do it. In Guatemala the mission was shaping up as a minuscule conventional military invasion, its CIA cloak-and-dagger underpinnings notwithstanding. The guardsmen were training the B-26 pilots to support a small-scale, WWII-style amphibious landing. In the cloud-covered mountains above Retalhuleu, the CIA had put together a miniature army equipped "with up-to-date weapons like bazookas, recoilless antitank guns and even a handful of medium tanks." Army special forces advisers were brought in to rush the Cuban recruits through paratrooper training and courses in conventional military tactics.[32] It was hard to think of the invasion as other than a conventional military operation except that it was run by the CIA, was to be carried out by Cuban exiles, and was being second-guessed all the way up the White House. The pulling of political strings at the highest levels gave the invasion a life not of its own, but one that continually changed right up to the eleventh hour before it was launched.

President Kennedy told Theodore Sorensen, his Special Counsel, that he had been astonished at the magnitude and daring of the Cuban plan from the time he was briefed on it as President-elect in

Palm Beach. From that moment on Kennedy had grave doubts about the CIA plan.[33] When he was formally briefed on January 28, none of the daring and magnitude was taken out. The plan called for a daytime landing on the south coast of central Cuba near Trinidad, a city of 18,000 people where anti-Castro activity was known to exist. If the invasion failed, the Cuban exiles could melt into the nearby Escambray Mountains and join resistance forces still holding out against Castro's army. How could the U.S. Government plausibly deny its involvement in an operation of this magnitude, the President wondered? The plan had the U.S. Government's handwriting all over it.

President Kennedy asked the Joint Chiefs of Staff to analyze the plan. Although General Gray believed the odds were stacked 70-30 against a favorable outcome, his report to the JCS had given the Trinidad Plan a "fair" chance of succeeding. In a joint session the individual service chiefs, the Marine Corps' General David M. Shoup among them, attacked the Trinidad Plan on the grounds that there were too many "ifs" involved. There was no reason to believe that the invasion would spark an uprising against Castro, who was a hero to the Cuban masses, or that a brigade-sized force could last more than a few days against Castro's superior numbers even if the invaders had total air superiority.[34]

Rather than raising these grave concerns, the report to the White House by the JCS chairman, General Lyman L. Lemnitzer, equivocated on the main points. Lemnitzer's memorandum of 3 February repeated Gray's assertion that the plan had a "fair" chance of ultimate success. Even if the invasion failed to achieve all of the objectives, Lemnitzer noted that it "could contribute to the eventual overthrow of the Castro regime." Although overt U.S. intervention would not necessarily be required, the chairman concluded that the invasion forces could not hold out against Castro's army for long, "lacking a popular uprising or substantial follow-on forces."[35]

Guatemalan P-51 Mustang fighter makes a low pass over Retalhuleu
(courtesy of Joe Shannon).

The JCS sent a military team of Army, Navy, and Air Force
officers to Guatemala near the end of February to report on the
effectiveness of the Cuban Expeditionary Force. The team's report
praised the combat readiness and morale of the Cuban brigade, but
noted that the visibility of activities at Retalhuleu and Puerto
Cabezas had raised the odds against achieving surprise to about 85-
to-15. The evaluation reemphasized the critical importance of
surprise and air superiority, warning that one Castro aircraft armed
with .50 caliber machine guns could sink the entire invasion force.[36]

Meanwhile, the administration had begun to give the Trinidad
Plan a slow and agonizing facelift. Originally the plan assigned a D-
Day of March 5 for the invasion. On February 17 President
Kennedy postponed the invasion when the agencies involved were
not responsive to his repeated concerns about the scope and
deniability of the operation. The President pressed for alternatives
to "a full-fledged invasion supported by U.S. planes and ships." He

asked why the brigade "could not . . . be landed gradually and quietly and make its first major military efforts from the mountains—then take shape as a Cuban force within Cuba, not as an invasion force sent by the Yankees?" The President informed the State Department, CIA, and Joint Chiefs of Staff that he favored "a more moderate approach, such as mass infiltration."[37]

Jake Esterline, head of the Cuban task force, said in retrospect that he believed the CIA should have stopped what it was doing on the invasion and given the new administration "time to develop their own options and think about how they might want to deal with this problem." Instead what the Agency essentially handed the administration was a *fait accompli*, what Allen Dulles described as "the disposal problem." It was difficult to back off from the fact that a force of 1,500 Cuban exiles was in the mountains of Guatemala itching for action, or that the governments of Guatemala and Nicaragua wanted the affair over and done with before it caused them political embarrassment. Other pressures included Castro's success in suppressing the resistance movement in Cuba and the daily arrival in Havana of massive arms shipments from the Soviet bloc nations. Soviet MiGs reportedly were in Havana waiting to be uncrated.[38]

Through February and March the President ordered changes to the invasion plans, amid conflicting opinions from the CIA, the Joint Chiefs of Staff, the State Department, the Congress, and other agencies. At a White House meeting on March 11 the President rejected the Trinidad Plan and sent Richard Bissell back to the drawing board. At the meeting Bissell had presented four alternative courses of action, but stuck to his advocacy of the CIA's position. Secretary of State Dean Rusk voiced strong opposition to the plan because it was too much like an invasion. Kennedy rejected the plan because it was "too noisy" and openly exposed the role of the United States. Insisting on plausible deniability of the government's role, he gave the CIA four days to come up with a "less spectacular" alternative. Bissell later wrote:

> It is hard to believe in retrospect that the president and his advisers felt the plans for a large-scale, complicated military operation that had been ongoing for more than a year could be reworked in four days and still offer a high likelihood of success. It is equally amazing that we in the agency agreed so rapidly.[39]

Bissell tasked Esterline and his paramilitary staff to rework the plan. Colonel Hawkins said they pored over maps and intelligence reports for two days and nights before settling on the Bay of Pigs as the only site that satisfied the White House's requirements. Located 100 miles west of Trinidad the Bay of Pigs did not make an ideal beachhead. The beach was surrounded by an impassable swamp and was too far away for the Escambray Mountains to serve as an escape route. There was an airfield near the small town of Giron, however, which could be captured on the first day for use by the B-26s. At Dean Rusk's urging the President wanted the B-26s to operate from an airfield in Cuba after the first day so the bombing raids would appear to be an internal affair. The agency also devised a scheme to have a B-26 with Cuban markings fly to Miami and pose as a defector to make it appear that Castro had been attacked by his own pilots.[40]

Called Zapata for the name of the peninsula where the Bay of Pigs was located, the revised plan was vetted by the JCS and McGeorge Bundy, Kennedy's national security adviser, before going to the President. Bissell briefed the President on the afternoon of March 15. The plan called for a dawn attack on Castro's airfields by 16 B-26s two days prior to landing the brigade at the Bay of Pigs, with follow-up strikes by the same number of bombers planned at first light on the morning of the invasion. The new landing site eased White House concerns about "attracting undue attention," but both the President and his national security adviser still found the air plan "too noisy." Kennedy wanted assurances that the landing operations would be carried out under the cover of darkness and the ships would be "clear of the area by dawn."[41]

The President approved the revised plan the following day with the understanding that the invasion could be called off up to twenty-four hours before D-Day. Bissell and his staff were still uneasy about the air plan for the invasion. While everyone seemed to understand that Castro's air force had to be taken out, the President asked repeatedly whether the air strikes were necessary. Bundy described the air plan as a "noisy enterprise." Colonel Beerli cautioned that "everyone was counting on the air arm to do more than it would be able to do." The bombers were going in unprotected, and Beerli knew that taking and securing an airfield near the beachhead was no easy task for the invading force.[42]

In the hectic weeks before the invasion, there were times when Kennedy's aides believed he would call off the invasion. The President was getting conflicting opinions from all sides, with members of his staff and Senator J. William Fulbright, chairman of the Senate Foreign Relations Committee, urging that the invasion be cancelled. Dogged by indecision and delays the deadline for the invasion slipped from April 5 to April 15, then finally to April 17. When White House aide Arthur Schlesinger asked Kennedy on March 28 what he thought "about this damned invasion," the President answered, "I think about it as little as possible."[43]

A sure sign the operation was in trouble came the week before the pre-invasion airstrikes that were planned for April 15. Jacob Esterline and Jack Hawkins, the two men below Bissell who were most responsible for planning and carrying out the invasion, had become increasingly concerned about the "uncertainty, indecision and lack of commitment" shown by the White House. On April 8, they went to Bissell's home and stated "unequivocally that an operation at the Bay of Pigs offered no hope of overthrowing Castro and was certain to end in disaster." They pointed out "that the brigade could neither hold a beachhead there against Castro's tanks and much larger infantry forces nor break out through the swamp and fight its way across eighty miles of flat, open country to the mountains." Bissell told the two men that it was too late to stop the invasion, that it would proceed with or without them. He promised to try and "persuade the president to allow us to conduct enough air operations to get rid of the Castro air force."[44]

At Puerto Cabezas the Cuban pilots and their American advisers, unaware of the task force's forewarning of failure or the political drama being played out in Washington, were getting ready to go. They had relocated from Retalhaleu two weeks before they were to launch the pre-invasion strikes on April 15. The infantry was

Pier at Puerto Cabezas, Nicaragua, where Brigade 2506 sailed for Cuba in April 1961 (courtesy of Joe Shannon).

The *Barbara J*, one of the "rust-bucket" merchant vessels used to support the Bay of Pigs invasion (courtesy of Joe Shannon).

transported to Puerto Cabezas in C-54s on the 14th and began boarding the merchant ships anchored about three miles from the base. The dilapidated invasion fleet consisted of two WWII-vintage landing craft, the *Blagar* and the *Barbara J*, and five rusty freighters that were registered in Havana and had Cuban crews. The freighters (the *Rio Escondido, Houston, Caribe, Atlantico,* and *Lake Charles*) were provided by Eduardo Garcia, the anti-Castro partner of a Cuban shipping line.[45]

The brigade commander, Jose "Pepe" San Roman, whose brother Roberto was one of the battalion commanders, sailed aboard the *Blagar* and led the brigade ashore at the start of the invasion. Also on board the *Blagar*, which served as a command ship, was the CIA task force chief Jake Esterline and Manuel Artime, the Revolutionary Council's representative to the brigade. Once the invasion achieved its objectives, the CIA's plans called for landing Miro Cardona and the council in Cuba to set up a provisional government. During the brigade's three days at sea, they passed near tiny Swan Island where a U.S. radio station broadcast coded messages to resistance fighters in Cuba and anti-Castro propaganda to the Cuban people.[46]

The Cuban pilots knew that the infantrymen were relying on their B-26 strikes to knock out Castro's air capability before going ashore on the 17th. The pilots were confident, but not cocky. They would have preferred having fighter escorts, but that had been ruled out because the older fighters available to them did not have the range required to fly with the bombers from Puerto Cabezas. Not having fighter cover made it imperative that Castro's air forces be destroyed. Otherwise, the B-26s were without air-to-air capability and could not survive against enemy fighters. If Castro's fighters were not taken out, however, the Cuban pilots and their advisers had faith that Navy jets aboard the carrier Essex would come to their rescue. Captain Ferrer recalled a poignant moment when he and Alabama adviser Wade Gray drove a jeep up the coast to watch the brigade sail for Cuba. Driving back to Happy Valley their conversation turned to the lack of fighter escort for the bombers. When Ferrer mentioned how defenseless the B-26 looked without tail guns, his friend's soft Alabama drawl reassured him there was nothing to worry about. Ferrer recalled:

Wade put his hand on my shoulder and said, "I know. I know. But don't worry. We're gonna have Cuban pilots who don't speak Spanish and who have blond hair and blue eyes taking care of us, and an aircraft carrier which is loaded with the latest model fighters. We can't lose!"[47]

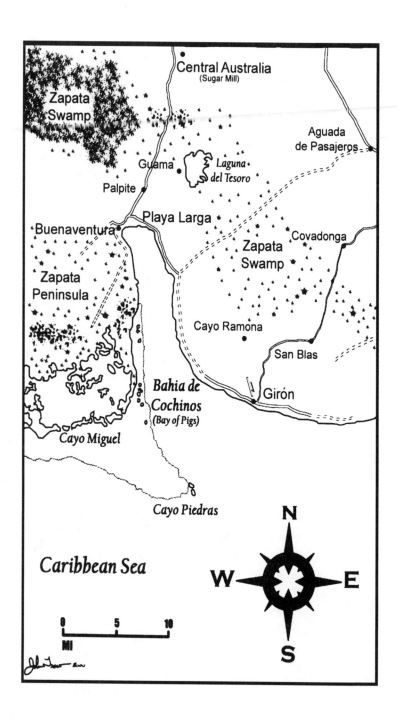

3

The Operation Begins

NO EXPERIENCE DRAWS fighting men closer than training together for war unless it is going together into the real thing. During the weeks of preparation at Retalhuleu the Cuban pilots and their U.S. advisors had grown close. Their occasional personal differences and misunderstandings had given way to the bonding that accompanies warriors into battle and follows them through life. The move to Puerto Cabezas in anticipation of the initial air strikes on the morning of April 15 drew them even closer. A feeling of anxiety had spread through the group during the final hours, however, as expressed by Edward Ferrer to his friend Wade Gray while watching the brigade set sail for Cuba. Their uneasiness grew out of an announcement at a pre-mission briefing that the strike force making the initial attack against Castro's airfields had been cut in half, from sixteen to eight aircraft.[1]

Not announced to the group at Puerto Cabezas was that the order to reduce the strike force had come from the White House. President Kennedy had called Richard Bissell on the day before the first raids were to take place and asked how many aircraft were involved. When Bissell stated that sixteen aircraft were scheduled for the mission, Kennedy said that was too many. He wanted the number reduced to a minimal effort to avoid the appearance of U.S. involvement. Bissell did not argue the point or explain to the President the critical importance of wiping out Castro's air forces before allowing the invasion to proceed. He arbitrarily reduced the strike force by half to comply with the President's guidance.[2]

At the briefing the Cuban pilots at Puerto Cabezas protested vehemently, but to no avail.[3] They knew that failing to get all of Castro's planes with the first strikes on the morning of the 15th would make the second ones more difficult and more dangerous. Forewarned, the Cuban air force would simply hide any remaining planes or would flush them to attack the incoming bombers. Second or third wave strikes against empty airfields could destroy facilities and crater runways, but these were easily repaired. Experienced airmen knew to throw everything they had into that all-important first strike and to follow up quickly before the enemy had time to recover. The arguments were heard at Puerto Cabezas, but not at the White House where they might have done some good.

Because of the long distance they had to fly, the B-26s were limited in the amount of time they had in the target area. The turrets on the B-26s were replaced with auxiliary tanks to give the bombers a total of about eight hours of fuel. Since the flight from Puerto Cabezas to Cuba was about three hours each way, the fuel supply allowed them only thirty minutes or so over the target. More fuel is consumed in combat than under normal conditions, and the pilots needed the extra hour and a half as a safety margin in case anything went wrong. There was no recovery base in the event the bombers could not make it back to Puerto Cabezas, but they could make an emergency landing in the Cayman Islands northwest of Jamaica. The crews were at a great disadvantage if they had to ditch because the B-26 would sink like an anvil.[4]

The misgivings Colonel Hawkins had about the invasion did not extend to the readiness of the brigade itself. After flying to

Nicaragua for the final briefing of brigade and battalion commanders before they sailed for Cuba, Hawkins reported that his confidence had grown while meeting with the commanders and observing the readiness of their forces. He was impressed by the officers who were "young, vigorous, intelligent and motivated with a fanatical urge to begin battle," and found the brigade to be well organized, more heavily armed and better equipped in some respects than U.S. infantry units. "This Cuban force is motivated, strong, well trained, armed to the teeth and ready," he concluded. "I believe profoundly that it would be a serious mistake for the United States to deter it from its intended purpose."[5]

Hawkins also said that he carefully observed air operations, noting that the aircraft "were kept with pride" and some of the B-26 crews were so eager to commence they had "already armed their aircraft." "Germosen informed me today that he considers the B-26 squadron equal to the best U.S. Air Force squadron," Hawkins stated.[6] Spirits were high at Puerto Cabezas despite concerns about the limited number of B-26s that could participate in the first day's strikes. Shannon had nothing but praise for the Cuban pilots. He said that in all his Air Force experience he had never known any pilots to compare with them. "The Cuban pilots were real tigers," he said. They were "fighting for their homeland," and were ready to go.[7] At the pre-mission briefing, the CIA air commander Gar read off the names of the eight pilots and eight navigators who were to fly the first mission. The crews were then moved to an isolation area to be briefed on their specific targets and to rest up for a predawn takeoff the next morning.[8]

The CIA commander picked a volunteer, Mario Zuniga, for the special mission that was intended to make the next day's airstrikes appear to be part of a rebellion against Castro by his own forces. Zuniga too was taken to the isolation area where an American adviser explained that his mission was to fly a B-26 to Florida and

Gustavo Ponzoa, former Cubana Airlines pilot, flew numerous B-26 strike missions in support of Bay of Pigs invasion (courtesy of Colonel Mike Haas, USAF Ret.).

land at Miami International Airport subsequent to the attacks on Cuban airfields. The B-26 was disguised with false Cuban air force markings and rigged to give the appearance it had suffered battle damage. Zuniga's cover story was that he was one of a group of pilots who had rebelled against Castro and that his plane had been damaged by ground fire while fleeing Cuba.[9]

Meanwhile the attacks on Castro's military airfields proceeded as planned. The first flight of two B-26s, piloted by Captains Gonzalo Herrera and Gustavo Ponzoa, took off at 2 a.m. The heavily armed bombers climbed to 8,000 feet and cruised northeast toward their target, Antonio Maceo Airport in the city of Santiago on Cuba's southeast coast. The other two flights, consisting of three B-26s each, took off soon afterward and flew due north toward two other Cuban air bases, Libertad west of Havana and San Antonio de los Banos to the south. Captains Jose Crespo, Daniel Fernandez-Mon, and Osvaldo Piedra were the pilots in the second flight. The pilots in the third flight were Captains Luis Cosme, Rene Garcia, and Alfredo Caballero. There was a navigator assigned to each plane. Their arrivals over the targets were synchronized so the dawn attacks were made simultaneously. [10]

Joe Shannon was the adviser to Herrera and Ponzoa, the two Cuban pilots who attacked the Santiago airfield. Herrera and Ponzoa encountered heavy ground fire and their bombers sustained battle damage, but the pilots completed their mission and returned safely to Puerto Cabezas. They inflicted heavy damage on the base. Ponzoa had been a transport pilot who flew out of Santiago and knew the area well. Shannon recalled that Ponzoa destroyed a C-47 he once had flown. He had instructed the pilots not to destroy the fuel dump since the field might be captured and used by the invasion forces, but said they destroyed everything in sight. The pilots reported that five enemy planes were destroyed in the Santiago attack. The other flights reported destroying half of Castro's offensive air capability at Libertad and seventy-five to eighty percent at San Antonio de los Banos. Aerial reconnaissance revealed, however, that eight aircraft comprising half of Castro's air force had escaped destruction.[11]

The three B-26s that attacked San Antonio de los Banos suffered surprisingly little battle damage and returned safely to Puerto Cabezas leaving flames and plumes of smoke behind them. The three B-26s attacking the heavily defended Libertad, which housed Cuba's air force headquarters, were not so fortunate. The bombers inflicted substantial damage, but came under heavy and accurate fire from antiaircraft weapons provided by Castro's allies in eastern Europe. After completing its runs on the target, one of the B-26s "exploded in a ball of fire and plunged into the sea." The pilot

Captain Daniel Fernandez-Mon and his navigator Gaston Perez were the first to die in the air battle over Cuba. A second B-26 expended its ordnance and made an emergency landing in the Cayman Islands before limping back to Puerto Cabezas full of bullet holes. The third B-26 flown by Captain Crespo lost an engine and diverted to Boca Chica Naval Air Station in Key West, Florida. The plane was quickly repaired and refueled for the return flight to Puerto Cabezas.[12]

Mario Zuniga, meanwhile, had landed at Miami International Airport and announced that he was defecting to the United States after he and other Cuban air force rebels had bombed Castro's military airfields. Miami reporters did not buy his story. A writer for *Time* reported that the pilot landed the crate "with an engine needlessly feathered and a cock-and-bull story that he had attacked the airfields." Other reporters noted that Zuniga's B-26 did not have a Plexiglas nose like those flown by the Cuban air force, and "that dust and undisturbed grease covered bomb-bay fittings, electrical connections to rocket mounts were corroded, guns were uncocked and unfired."[13]

The discrepancies in Zuniga's story were not made known to Adlai Stevenson, the U.S. Ambassador to the United Nations, however, when he addressed the General Assembly in response to Cuba's claims that the United States was responsible for the bombing attacks. The former presidential candidate had not even been told that the U.S. Government was behind the bombings. Stevenson showed a photograph of Zuniga's B-26 to support his denial of U.S. involvement. The Cuban Foreign Minister pointed out that the B-26 in the photograph was not the same as those owned by his country. At the White House, Ambassador Stevenson's embarrassment was of little consequence considering that the CIA's careless handling of the B-26 ruse had blown the cover on the U.S. Government's role in the invasion before it ever started.[14]

WITHIN THE CIA TASK FORCE and at Puerto Cabezas, the main concern was the eight Cuban aircraft that were still operational after the early morning strikes on the 15th. These eight planes, an assortment of B-26s, Sea Furies and T-33 jets, posed a deadly threat to the invasion force and its supporting aircraft. The men at Puerto Cabezas were certain that this threat could have been removed had the full complement of sixteen B-26s been authorized to participate in the pre-invasion strikes. Reducing the strike force on the 15th and cancelling the cleanup strikes that were to follow put the invasion in serious jeopardy. Additional strikes were planned in support of the invasion on the morning of the 17th, but the element of surprise was lost. Castro reportedly had ordered his pilots to sleep under the wings of their planes and be ready to scramble when the siren sounded.[15]

At Puerto Cabezas the returning pilots were shocked to hear that no more strikes were authorized until the morning of the 17th when Brigade 2506 was scheduled to make its landing at the Bay of Pigs. The men waiting on the ground were saddened by the news that Danny Fernandez-Mon and Perez would not be coming back. Bobby Whitley described Fernandez-Mon as "friendly, outgoing, and a good ol' boy. He was the only person with a record player and he would leave it at the 'Airport Inn' with his records so we could play it when he wasn't around," Whitley recalled. "He was killed the first day. It hit us hard. He was well liked."[16]

There were to be more casualties because the air strikes were reduced on the 15th and the follow-up strikes scheduled for the next two days were cancelled. These decisions were an omen that things could get worse, and they did—starting just hours before the landing was to begin at the Bay of Pigs. Colonel Jack Hawkins was in the CIA operations center known as Quarters Eye around 10 p.m. on April 16, the night before the invasion, when Jake Esterline rushed in and informed him that the President had canceled the air strikes that were planned against Castro's airfields at first light the next morning. National Security Adviser McGeorge Bundy had telephoned General Cabell to advise him that the air strikes were cancelled and that no more strategic strikes were to be flown until the landing forces seized the Cuban airstrip and the B-26s were operating from Cuban soil. The bombers were ordered to fly only missions that were in direct support of the invasion forces.[17]

The B-26 pilots at Puerto Cabezas were in the cockpits of their planes when the order came down canceling the strategic strikes against the Cuban airfields. Joe Shannon said the Cuban pilots and the advisers were devastated. Captain Ferrer wrote in his book *Operation Puma* that Reid Doster's reaction spoke for everyone at Puerto Cabezas. He recalled that Doster cursed the Washington bureaucrats, slammed his cap to the ground in anger, and roared, "There goes the fucking war!"[18]

The reactions from Esterline and Hawkins were stronger even than Reid Doster's outburst on the flightline at Puerto Cabezas. They were appalled that the White House had denied the brigade a last opportunity to finish off Castro's aircraft on the ground and gain control of the air over the beachhead. Bissell wrote in his memoirs that Hawkins hit the table with his fist and cursed angrily when told about the cancelled air strikes. "Goddamn it, this is criminal negligence," Hawkins yelled. Esterline was equally demonstrative in venting his anger. General Cabell was more soldierly, taking the position that the task force had been given its marching orders and had to get on with the job.[19]

Hawkins stated that he and Esterline warned their superiors of the dire consequences for the invasion if they were not authorized to attack the aircraft as planned. It had been only a week since the two men threatened to resign because of the constraints placed on military planning for the invasion and the situation was getting worse, not better. At their urging Cabell and Bissell met with

Secretary of State Dean Rusk, who had advocated cancelling the air strikes, and made a halfhearted attempt to have the decision reversed. Rusk discussed their concerns with the President, who was away from Washington, but stuck to the State Department's position that the air strikes should not go forward. He offered the telephone to Cabell and Bissell so the CIA's position could be argued directly to the President, but they declined. The President stood firm on his decision to cancel the airstrikes. At that point, Hawkins said, "The Cuban Brigade was doomed."[20]

IN VIEW OF THE PRIORITY given to denying the U.S. Government's role, what would have been the decibel levels coming from the White House had it been known that two Americans were going ashore with Brigade 2506 and that one of them would fire the first shot of the ground battle? Grayston L. Lynch, a retired U.S. Army Special Forces officer who later wrote a gripping firsthand account of the invasion, recalled that he and another CIA agent William "Rip" Robertson were left out of the plans because no one in the upper echelons knew they would be aboard the ships. Sailing into the mouth of Cochinos Bay aboard the command ship *Blagar* after midnight on April 17, Lynch and six Cuban frogmen went ashore in a rubber raft near the town of Giron. Robertson, who was aboard the *Barbara J*, made a similar recon landing at Playa Larga. When a militia outpost challenged them, Lynch and the frogmen fired their machine guns and automatic rifles killing the militiamen. The battle for the Bay of Pigs was underway.[21]

Lynch recalled that before Brigade 2506 set sail from Puerto Cabezas on April 14, a CIA team led by Colonel Hawkins had flown down from Washington to brief them. At the briefing, the team had assured the landing forces that they had nothing to fear from Castro's planes. "No Castro planes will get off the ground," the briefer said. Lynch also recalled the "wild cheering" aboard the

Blagar when news came that the B-26s had attacked the Cuban airfields, and then "the sudden sinking sensation" in the pit of his stomach upon hearing that the follow-on strikes were canceled because of "political considerations." A battle-hardened veteran of World War II, Korea, and special forces actions in Laos, Lynch knew that "whoever controlled the air over Cochinos Bay controlled Cuba."[22]

Coming ashore in waves behind the frogmen the brigade's main forces hit the beaches at Giron, an open area to the east of Giron, and at the far end of the bay near the small resort village of Playa Larga. Sporadic firefights involving Castro's militiamen broke out across the three landing areas, with the heaviest resistance occurring further inland north of Playa Larga. Well before sunrise the brigade had captured Giron and the small airfield that was to be used by their planes. Landing at night presented unique problems for the brigade, however, and the unloading of men and equipment was still underway when the first rays from the sun broke over the Sierra de Trinidad mountain peaks to the east.[23]

A diversionary landing of 160 men was to have taken place thirty miles east of the U.S. Navy base at Guantanamo Bay, but was aborted two nights running for tactical reasons. The success that a feint using rubber rafts with radios simulating battle sounds had in diverting Castro's attention temporarily away from the main landing area suggested that the larger diversionary tactic might have helped had it been carried out as planned.[24]

As the landings got underway at Cochinos Bay, six transports (five C-46 Commandos and one C-54 Skymaster) timed their departure from Puerto Cabezas to arrive over the beachhead at daybreak. Upon reaching their targets the transports had orders to drop thirty paratroopers each with weapons and equipment at predesignated coordinates around the outer perimeters of the landing zones. Edward Ferrer was at the controls of one of the C-46s on

Captain Edward Ferrer at the controls of a C-46 Commando cargo aircraft. Ferrer flew continuous missions during the Bay of Pigs dropping paratroopers, equipment, and ammunition (courtesy of Captain Ferrer).

the 17th. He recalled that the transport pilots had to take great care to drop the paratroopers "on or very close to the roads, because they had been constructed on the most solid area of Zapata Swamp." Ferrer also flew low over the small landing field west of Giron to make certain that the runway was operational.[25]

No sooner had the transports cleared the runway at Puerto Cabezas than flights of heavily armed B-26s followed them into the night sky. Orders had come from Washington that the bombers could fly air support for the men on the ground at the Bay of Pigs, but could not strike strategic targets. The plan called for the bombers to begin operating from Cuban soil once the airfield near Giron was secure. One or two transport aircraft did land there for a brief period, but the situation in the air and on the battlefield deteriorated too quickly for Giron to ever serve as a base of operations for the brigade's bombers or transports. Roy Wilson was in a C-46 that landed at Giron and dropped off troops and ammunition. Asked how long they were there, he exclaimed: "Ten minutes. We got our ass out of there."[26]

Four B-26s flew cover for the paratrooper drops and struck targets of opportunity before having to return to Puerto Cabezas. When other flights of B-26s began to arrive over the beaches the Cuban army had moved into the forward area to counter the invasion and Cuban planes had taken to the skies to attack the beachhead and the cargo ships anchored offshore. Since the brigade's B-26s were painted with Cuban colors, the invasion forces could

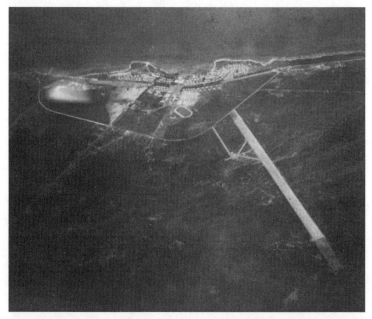

Aerial view of the airstrip at Giron. Brigade 2506 captured the airstrip on the first day of the invasion, but could not hold it (courtesy of Joe Shannon).

not distinguish between friendly and enemy planes until they started coming under fire. Pilots of both bombers and transports reported being fired at as they flew low over their own forces. One of the C-46s was hit by friendly fire as it passed over Giron to drop paratroopers.[27]

The brigade B-26s made a gallant effort to drive Castro's planes away from the beachhead, but they were no match for the fighters. Unable to operate out of Giron the bombers were shuttling back and forth between Nicaragua and Cuba, attempting to provide continuous air cover over the beachhead, while Castro's planes merely recovered at their home bases to quickly return, refueled and rearmed, to the skies unimpeded. The brigade's aircrews—under constant attack and flying continuously into combat on the 17th—were worn out. Even Mario Zuniga who flew the phony B-26 to Miami on April 15 was back at Puerto Cabezas flying his share of the missions. The ground crews at Puerto Cabezas, where equipment and conditions were primitive at best, worked around the clock to rearm the bombers with close air support munitions and to keep the planes in the air.

As dawn broke over Cochinos Bay the brigade came under sudden and continuous attacks from Castro's planes. Gunners on the command ship *Blagar* brought down a Cuban B-26 and Castro also lost a Sea Fury to ground fire, but the enemy's few remaining planes lashed out at the invasion forces with devastating results. Two of the brigade's ships, the *Houston* and the *Rio Escondido*, with their precious cargos of ammunition and aviation fuel were put out of action.[28] A Sea Fury flew over the *Houston* and reported that it was lying "like a big mortally wounded fish" in the bay. The Sea Fury then attacked the *Rio Escondido*, hitting the freighter dead center with rockets.[29]

There were countless acts of bravery on the surface and in the air. From a front-row seat on the *Blagar* Grayston Lynch cursed two "arrogant bastards" in T-33s who performed victory rolls after destroying their targets. He observed men in small boats from the other ships going to the rescue of seamen on the *Rio Escondido* after the first explosion, and he marveled at their courage because "they knew the ship was a veritable bomb." Then he saw the freighter rocked by a secondary explosion that resembled "a huge, mushroom-shaped fireball." He wrote:

> The mushroom spread until it was over a mile in diameter and several thousand feet high. As it slowly lifted from the water, the stem was exposed, giving it the appearance of a nuclear explosion. The cloud continued to rise. As the mushroom stem lifted off the water, a portion of the ship's capsized stern was briefly visible. Slowly it slid out of sight, one twisted propeller still turning.[30]

Captain Ferrer, in his book *Operation Puma*, tells a wonderful story about an elderly priest who pleaded to fly with him on a perilous C-46 mission back to Giron on the 17th. Too weary to argue after flying all day Ferrer finally gave in to the priest's impassioned pleas, but only after he promised to use an M-3 rifle Ferrer handed him. Packed with ammunition the overloaded C-46 was a flying bomb if hit by ground fire or enemy planes. A B-26 escort had to turn back because of problems with the auxiliary fuel tanks and jammed guns. The C-46 arrived over Giron, but was unable to land because T-33 fighters were attacking in the area. Turning back over the water toward Puerto Cabezas, Ferrer breathed a sigh of relief when two Douglas A-4 jet fighters with U.S. Navy markings zoomed past them. He was shocked back to reality when all hell broke loose from the back of the C-46 where the hold was crammed with explosives. Two crewmen and the old priest were wildly shooting out of the open door and windows at the A-4s. Ferrer said the old priest was kneeling at the window firing the M-

3 "like a crazy man." They had to be stopped immediately, Ferrer said, not because the Navy jets were in danger—they had already gone past the C-46—but because he was afraid they "would accidentally shoot off one of our wings."[31]

When Castro's planes destroyed the *Houston* and the *Rio Escondido* the other ships, under withering fire from the T-33s and Sea Furies, had to withdraw out to sea without unloading all the troops they were carrying or their cargo. The ships had orders to rendezvous 50 miles off the coast but two freighters, the *Atlantico* and the *Caribe*, headed south without stopping until intercepted by the U.S. Navy. As dusk settled over Cochinos Bay the brigade still held the beachhead and the access roads despite their heavy losses from the air attacks. Without waiting for dawn the Cuban army seized the initiative by moving reinforcements, including tanks and artillery, into the forward area as firefights continued through the night.[32]

There was no doubt who dominated the skies as the sun set on the first day of the invasion. Castro's tiny air force numbering less than eight aircraft and no more than ten airmen had clearly won the day. It lost two planes to ground fire, but had shot down four of the invasion air force's B-26s killing six airmen and severely wounding another. One navigator bailed out of his burning plane and was picked up by the destroyer *USS Murray*. A fifth B-26 crashed into the coastal jungles of Nicaragua killing the pilot and navigator.[33] Adding the B-26 that was lost during the airfield strikes on the 15th, the brigade air force was down to ten bombers, some of which needed patching up. More devastating was the loss of aircrews, depleting a small force already demoralized and dead-tired from continuous combat in skies dominated by enemy fighters.

At Puerto Cabezas the ground crews' grueling jobs of repairing the bombers and rearming them for their next missions had worn the men to a frazzle. "We had a terrible workload," Lou Hudson recalled. "It was go, go, go during the strikes. I went three days and nights without sleep." Don Crocker fell asleep under a B-26 nose. Another B-26 taxied by and threw gravel all over Crocker without waking him. Hudson said he went to the flight surgeon, Doctor Theodore Marrs (an Air Guard pediatrician with a practice in Montgomery, Alabama) to get something to help him sleep. Marrs told him to take an aspirin.[34] Apparently the doctor saved the stronger sedatives for the pilots who were flying the missions. Ferrer said Marrs gave him a tiny pill to help him sleep after a mission on the 17th, only to have him take another pill to keep him awake two hours later when he had to make another run to Cuba.[35] As the pilots and crews grabbed what little sleep they could on that tortured tropical night, there was no time for what the day's battle had wrought, only thoughts of what tomorrow would bring.

4

The Invasion's Final Hours

O N TUESDAY THE 18TH THE CIA got authority for American contract crews to fly B-26s into the air battle.[1] The
situation at Cochinos Bay was "not a bit good,"
McGeorge Bundy reported to President Kennedy, and had deteriorated to the point that bolder measures short of overt U.S. military
action would not likely turn the tide. Not one for hyperbole the
President's special assistant for national security affairs summarized
the situation: "The Cuban armed forces are stronger, the popular
response is weaker, and our tactical position is feebler than we had
hoped."[2]

When the President met with the special group on Cuba, Bissell
pressed hard for the use of U.S. air power. He specifically asked for
U.S. Navy carrier aircraft to fly cover for the B-26s. Bundy had
alerted the President to "expect other pleas in rapid crescendo"
because the invasion forces "are up against a formidable enemy, who
is reacting with military knowhow and vigor." Nevertheless, Bundy
supported the CIA's immediate request, believing even at this late
date the right course of action was "to eliminate the Castro air force,
by neutrally-painted U.S. planes if necessary, and then let the battle
go its way."[3]

77

Admiral Arleigh Burke urged the President to grant the CIA's request for naval air support. Earlier President Kennedy had authorized Admiral Burke to position U.S. Navy destroyers and the aircraft carrier *Essex* in international waters fifty miles off Cuba as a contingency measure. The carrier had aircraft ready, and Burke wanted to use them to clean out Castro's tanks and planes. Secretary of State Rusk advised the President to stick by his guns and not get U.S. forces involved in the conflict. Kennedy agreed with Rusk, but made minor concessions on the use of air power as the day wore on. It was a harrowing day for the White House, wrote the authors of a haunting postmortem on the Bay of Pigs, but "it was calamitous for 1,500 or so men who were clinging like crabs to a tiny patch of Cuban shoreline."[4]

THE GUIDANCE RECEIVED by the air commander at Puerto Cabezas on the 18th offered a glimmer of hope. A message from CIA headquarters authorized American contract crews to fly the B-26s on armed reconnaissance missions in support of ground forces, with the provision that they operate over the beachhead and sea approaches only. The message authorized American transport pilots to fly resupply drops over the beachhead during the hours of darkness. The American crews were cautioned that they "must not fall into enemy hands." The CIA instructed the crews that if an American was captured, despite all precautions, the U.S. Government would regard them as hired mercenaries and would deny any knowledge of their actions.[5]

The CIA arranged for four replacement B-26s to be flown to Puerto Cabezas from Eglin Air Force Base, Florida, and got approval for unmarked North American F-51 Mustangs to support the Cuban exiles from Giron if the airfield was operational and still under friendly control. The famous World War II fighters were redesignated from P-51s to F-51s before their introduction into the

Korean War in the fall of 1950. The propeller-driven fighters, which were retired from the Air National Guard in 1957, could not operate from Nicaragua because of their limited range. For the first time since the pre-invasion strikes on the 15th, the B-26s were authorized to attack strategic targets to eliminate Castro's air capability. The attacks on Cuban airfields were to be flown only at night by Cuban crews.[6]

During the predawn hours of the 18th a flight of four B-26s, having taken off from Puerto Cabezas just after midnight, arrived over the southeastern coast of Cuba to attack the San Antonio de los Banos airfield. Their mission was a desperate attempt to destroy Castro's few remaining warplanes. Unable to find the target because the base was blacked out and blanketed by haze, the bombers aborted the mission and flew armed reconnaissance against targets of opportunity before departing the area. Gonzalo Herrera (El Tigre) was one of the aircraft commanders and reported they were unable to find lucrative secondary targets because of the cloud cover. He and the other pilots tried tactics to draw enemy fire so they could pinpoint the gun batteries, but were unsuccessful. They returned to Puerto Cabezas in frustration.[7]

As the haze cleared over the Bay of Pigs that dreary morning the brave and battered warriors of Brigade 2506 were holding on, but were badly outnumbered and running out of ammunition. None of the transport planes got clearance to land at Giron on the 18th, and the merchant ships that withdrew from the coastal waters the day before were still out to sea. Grayston Lynch, aboard the *Blagar*, reported numerous problems getting the shiploads of ammunition back to the waiting troops on the beachhead. The least of these problems was a mutiny by the merchant seamen whom the men from the *Blagar* had rescued from the sinking *Rio Escondido* the previous day. The frightened seamen balked at returning to Cochinos Bay to be sunk a second time. Lynch said the mutiny lasted about five minutes before the *Blagar's* Cuban frogmen overpowered the merchant seamen and tossed them in the brig.[8]

After rounding up the ships and returning to the coastal waters off Cuba, the task force commander aboard the *Blagar* made radio contact with the brigade commander Jose "Pepe" San Roman at Giron to advise him that ammunitions and supplies were on their way. He congratulated Pepe for the victory at Playa Larga the day before. The brigade commander cursed and advised that the troops who fought at Playa Larga were now at Giron because they had run out of ammunition. Grayston Lynch got on the radio to assure the tough Cuban leader that ammunition would be brought in after nightfall and to pass on information that American jets were coming.[9]

The *Blagar* had received a message not to fire on four unmarked jets that were set to arrive over the beaches late that morning because they would be from the carrier *Essex.* Believing the Navy was finally coming to the brigade's rescue, the men experienced a rush of adrenaline when the silver jets streaked in low over the beachhead, then felt a huge letdown when the planes returned minutes later heading toward the open sea. Lynch contacted the carrier *Essex* and learned the overflight was a onetime reconnaissance mission, not the arrival of U.S. air power as hoped. "A moment later Castro's planes came in behind them, bombing and strafing the brigade's positions as though nothing had changed," Lynch wrote.[10]

At midday on the 18th two American B-26 pilots flew into battle with the brigade air force for the first time. The two Americans, Connie Siegrith and Doug Price, were full-time CIA contract pilots who volunteered for the mission. They knew that most of the Cuban crews, who had been flying continuously since the morning of the 17th, were in no condition to fly combat. The Americans had orders not to press their attacks too far inland over Cuba where they ran a greater risk of being shot down. While reluctantly authorizing the use of American pilots, the White House did not want to chance one of them being killed or captured by Castro's militia.[11]

Three flights of two B-26s each took off from Puerto Cabezas during the early afternoon of the 18th. The bombers flown by the Americans Doug and Sieg made up one flight. The aircraft commanders in the other two flights were names already familiar to anyone monitoring the air battle over Cuba: Captains Gustavo Ponzoa, Rene Garcia, Antonio Soto, and Mario Zuniga, who had flown the disguised B-26 to Miami on the 15th. Armed with napalm, rockets and machine guns, the B-26s arrived in staggered formations over the beachhead during the late afternoon. The timing was right because there were no enemy fighters in the skies to challenge the bombers and they caught Castro's troops and convoys in the open rolling down the road toward Giron.[12]

By the time Cuban fighters responded to the militia's call for air support, the six bombers had ripped into the columns of Soviet tanks and trucks, had expended all their ordnance, and were on their way back to Puerto Cabezas. Captain Ferrer, in his book *Operation Puma*, described the results:

> . . . there remained only smoking twisted wreckage. Hundreds of bodies were strewn along both sides of the buckled roadway.
>
> According to a communique published by the enemy, there were 900 casualties, and thirty vehicles were totally destroyed. But to no avail—the enemy kept advancing. Six hours later, another column opened a path through the wreckage and continued toward Red Beach.[13]

Coming in behind the B-26 strikes, Captain Ferrer led a flight of three C-54s low over the beachhead to airdrop desperately needed ammunition and supplies to the besieged brigade. Heavy fighting around Giron indicated to the pilots that Castro's forces were closing in on the beachhead. They arrived back at Puerto Cabezas to learn that the plan to bring in four F-51 Mustangs to the Giron airfield tō support the brigade had to be cancelled. Three F-51s lent to the CIA at Puerto Cabezas by the Nicaraguan government were of no use either. As night fell over their beloved Cuba the battered heroes of Brigade 2506 were being driven inexorably toward the coral floors offshore or the mangrove swamps of the Zapata Peninsula, for there was no escape route to the Escambray Mountains from Bahia de Cochinos.[14]

Seven Alabama guardsmen volunteered that evening when the CIA air commander at Puerto Cabezas told them that American pilots and crews were needed to fly B-26 sorties in support of the beleaguered brigade the next morning. After nightfall on the 18th word got around when the bombers and transports returned from their missions that the brigade, badly outnumbered and running out of ammunition, was barely holding on at Giron. This was backed up by messages from CIA headquarters. While the brigade was expected to make it through the night, Castro's forces had the escape routes cut off and were massing for an all-out attack after sunrise. Other Air Guard pilots wanted to go on the critical support mission the next morning but were either needed to fly cargo into the beachhead or were not experienced enough to fly the B-26s into combat.[15]

Joe Shannon and Riley Shamburger had been staying close to the operations shack monitoring the brigade's situation as best they could and were aware that the invaders were in desperate straits. The guardsmen had become close friends with the Cuban pilots during the grueling weeks of preparing for combat while in Guatemala. They knew their comrades were worn out. Without hesitation Shannon and Shamburger agreed to fly the mission along with fellow pilots Billy Goodwin and Pete Ray. "We did it for the

Cubans," Shannon told Associated Press writer David Langford, "but we knew it was over." Four other Alabamians (Leo Baker, Nick Sudano, Wade Gray, and James Vaughn) volunteered to go along as crew members. El Tigre Herrera and Mario Zuniga, who had been flying steadily since the 15th, refused to stand down from the mission.[16]

The six B-26s took off in staggered formations from the jungle airstrip at Puerto Cabezas during the early morning hours of the 19th. Just before the bombers taxied to the runway a message arrived from CIA headquarters that the Navy would provide one hour of air cover for the B-26s at dawn and the pilots should use the opportunity to attack Cuban forces on the approaches to the airfield. While Shannon and the other pilots spotted Navy jets with their U.S. markings painted over, the planes did not engage in the action. Rear Admiral John Clark, the on-site commander aboard the *Essex*, reported launching A-4D Skyhawks to provide air cover for the B-26s, but stated that the bombers had already departed the target area before their arrival.[17]

No acceptable explanation has been given for the failure to provide fighter cover on the 19th. Historian Arthur M. Schlesinger, Jr., wrote that a mix-up between the Nicaraguan and Cuban time zones resulted in the B-26s arriving over the beachhead an hour ahead of their jet support. Admiral Clark admitted that there was a misunderstanding as to times and that the B-26s passed over the *Essex* an hour early. He said the A-4Ds were launched immediately, but by the time they arrived over the beachhead the bombers had made their strikes and left. Author Peter Wyden wrote in 1979 that the skipper of the *Essex*, Captain S.S. "Pete" Searcy, complied with an order to burn "all orders and logs covering the time of the operation," but did not say who gave the order. The Navy acknowledged that the ship's log for April was missing and presumably lost.[18]

Whatever the explanation the B-26s—conducting their strikes without air cover—"ran into sharp enemy fire, and four Americans were killed." Billy Goodwin and Gonzalo Herrera reached the target area first and completed their strikes before Castro's T-33s had time to react. They dropped napalm and strafed a convoy of tanks and other military vehicles before turning back. El Tigre continued to press the attack against the convoy when Goodwin had to leave the target area with jammed .50 caliber machine guns and a hung rocket. After repeated attempts to dislodge the rocket failed, Goodwin landed at Puerto Cabezas with sparks flying from the rocket hanging nose down beneath the plane. Breathing a sigh of relief when the rocket did not explode, Goodwin thanked God it was not the napalm that got hung up.[19]

Bill Gray and Glenn Monaghan were manning a fire truck near the runway when they got word that Dodo Goodwin was coming in for a landing with hung ordnance. Gray said the ordnance was hanging 12 to 15 inches below the fuselage. The firemen were on the radio to General Doster as they drove beside Goodwin's B-26 "down the runway at the tip of his wing." Gray described the incident:

> ... Papa kept saying 'Get closer, get closer.' We didn't know if it was napalm or not. If it was and exploded on landing it would have killed us all. I was as close as I wanted or needed to be and was very thankful Dodo made a very soft 'marshmallow' landing. He greased that thing in. It was about as hairy a moment as I ever had in firefighting.[20]

There was more on Goodwin's mind than his own safety as he climbed down from the cockpit and strode to the operations shack. On the way back to Puerto Cabezas he heard Riley Shamburger shout over the radio that his plane was hit and on fire. Then he heard Joe Shannon's voice saying that a T-33 got Riley. Shannon and Shamburger had strafed a line of trucks on the coastline highway and pulled up over the water when the T-33s jumped them. The sun was low on the horizon, and when he heard Riley's frantic radio transmission Shannon looked to his left "just in time to see a T-33 coming out of the sun and firing at him." Shannon's fighter pilot instincts took over as he observed Shamburger's plane "hit the water a few hundred yards offshore." He violently turned into the oncoming T-33—his only logical option. With eight 50-caliber guns pointed directly at him, the T-33 pulled up sharply into a near-vertical climb. Shannon continued the left turn, flying as low as he could and at full throttle, and headed into the sun. After about fifteen or twenty miles he turned south, sighting two unmarked U.S. Navy AD-4s heading north as he gained altitude for the return flight to Puerto Cabezas.[21]

Willie Colvert was on the flightline when Shannon and Sudano landed. "They had flown so low we could still see seawater dripping down from the wheel wells and engine nacelle," Colvert recalled.[22] When Sudano stepped down from the plane, the first thing he had to do was "take a leak." General Doster came strolling up with his hands in his pockets while Sudano was urinating. "He came up too fast and too close and I splattered his boots," Sudano recalled, adding impishly, "Now, you know it was an accident." It was a fitting end to a bad mission. "I still get choked up over seeing Riley Shamburger and Wade Gray go down," he said.[23]

Shamburger and Gray were both killed when their plane crashed into the water. Further inland over the Australia Sugar Mill northwest of Giron another tragedy was unfolding. Pete Ray was low on fuel, but pressed the attack against targets near the sugar mill where Castro had his field headquarters. The other B-26 pilots received a Mayday transmission from Ray that his plane was under attack by an enemy fighter. The T-33 scored a direct hit on Ray's plane

Brigade 2506 commander Jose "Pepe" San Roman and Fidel Castro shown together after the brigade's defeat at the Bay of Pigs.

causing it to crash onto an open field near the sugar plantation several miles inland. Witnesses reported that Ray and Baker survived the crash, but were shot by Castro's soldiers. Buck Persons recalled there was a broadcast from Havana that day boasting about shooting down a B-26 and recovering the two bodies. Persons said he felt a sudden chill. "For the first time since we left Birmingham I felt the full impact of the fact that we were not playing games, that this was for real," he added in a somber voice.[24]

Persons and some of the young Cuban pilots were getting ready to fly the unmarked Nicaraguan F-51s to Cuba when they were told to scrub the mission, because the fighters could not land at Giron. Persons later admitted that it probably was for the best. It had been nineteen years since he had flown the Mustang during World War

II, and the first time the young Cubans had seen one up close. "I could see that we were not going to be the greatest bunch of tigers that had ever taken to the air," Persons said. "In fact, I began to wonder if we would not be more of a threat to one another than a major threat to Castro."[25]

Persons had his mind made up to fly that day, so when the F-51 mission was scrubbed he agreed to take a C-54 to Cochinos Bay on a drop mission. While he was getting a crew together for the flight, a message came in announcing that the invasion was over, that Castro had won. The Alabama guardsmen went back to their tents and packed up their dead comrades' personal belongings. They took the deaths hard. The mood inside the tents was like a mausoleum. The beer was warm and bitter to the taste. "What the hell happened?" Persons recalled someone asking.[26]

The Alabama Guard was a close-knit group. Joe Shannon and Riley Shamburger had been friends since they first joined the Birmingham unit after World War II. Buck Persons remembered his friend Shamburger as "a highly-skilled test pilot" who was "gregarious, fun-loving and hell-raising" and who "inspired confidence, loyalty and affection from his men." Roy Wilson had recruited his cousin Wade Gray for the CIA operation, not realizing that combat missions might be involved. Persons and Leo Baker had become friends working together at Retalhuleu. CMSgt Bobby Whitley and a couple of other guardsmen had grown up with Pete Ray and Wade Gray, and they had attended Tarrant High School near the Birmingham Airport together. Before flying the mission Ray gave Whitley his wallet and identification papers but kept his money, saying "I might need it to buy a drink in Havana."[27] Spirits were low at Puerto Cabezas that night. It had been a long day at the jungle staging base, but longer still for the Cuban patriots being rounded up with their hands in the air on the bloodstained sands of Cochinos Bay.

Fidel Castro looks over the wreckage of the B-26 Invader shot down
near his field headquarters on the final day of the Cuban invasion.
Thomas "Pete" Ray and Leo Baker survived the crash, but were killed
by Cuban soldiers (courtesy of Colonel Mike Haas, USAF Ret.).

WHEN GRAYSTON LYNCH talked by radio with Pepe San Roman at
midday on the 19th, he said they would go in and evacuate the
brigade if things got too rough. San Roman replied that the brigade
would not leave the island, but would fight to the end if they had to.
He was running out of ammunition at the time, and Castro's forces
were closing in. Two hours later the brigade headquarters was under
fire and men were fighting on the beach and in the water. San
Roman's last transmission stated that he was destroying his maps
and equipment because Castro's tanks had broken through and
were converging on the headquarters. "The radio went silent,"
wrote Lynch. "It was over."[28]

The brigade had fought bravely, even brilliantly some experts
said. As demonstrated early in a key battle for Rotunda de Playa

Larga, where three roads joined the coastal highway, the brigade's soldiers put up a ferocious fight against superior odds. Less than fifty men forming a roadblock at the rotunda held off 1,000 of Castro's men all day Monday and through the night before being forced to withdraw after sunrise Tuesday morning. Erneido Olivia, second in command to San Roman, called the battle "the night of the heroes." It was the heaviest fighting of the invasion.[29]

Lyman B. Kirkpatrick, Jr., who conducted the Inspector General's survey of the Cuban Operation in October 1961, estimated that San Roman's men, aided by the B-26s flying from Nicaragua, inflicted ten to one casualties on the other side in the three-day conflict. Approximately 1,500 Cuban exiles were pitted against Castro's 20,000 regulars with another 80,000 men in reserve. In addition to the warplanes that survived the airfield attacks, Castro's infantry was supported by Russian-made artillery, antiaircraft guns, and as many as 100 tanks against five that the invaders got ashore. The brigade suffered 103 casualties, including fourteen Cuban and American airmen. Castro's forces took 1,189 prisoners. At least two dozen men were rescued by CIA operatives and the U.S. Navy. The remaining hundred or so men were unaccounted for.[30]

While the CIA got ready to close out operations at Puerto Cabezas, Captain Ferrer and a crew of nine flew one final transport mission on April 20. The C-54 lifted off at dusk with a 10,000-pound load of supplies and weapons that were to be airdropped to a small group of partisans in the Sierra Maestra Mountains. Four hours later Ferrer's plane arrived over the drop-zone, located on the northern side of Pico Turquino, the tallest mountain in Cuba. Instead of signal lights from the partisans the C-54 ran into heavy antiaircraft fire from Castro's guns and had to turn back. Ferrer thought of dropping the weapons to lighten his aircraft and increase the rate of climb, but decided against giving Castro more free arms. He flew over the Turquino peak and dove toward the coastline, levelling off at 4,000 feet. Ferrer recalled that he was emotionally and physically drained flying back to Puerto Cabezas from "this, the last mission of our war."[31]

The morale of the Alabama guardsmen was at rock bottom after the death of their comrades and the tragic end to the invasion on the 19th. James Glenn stated with conviction that he and the other guardsmen believed strongly in what they were doing, that it was the right thing and was something that had to be done. "We were not allowed to do what was right. We were not allowed to win," he said. "The aircraft were there and ready to go. We had the means to do the job. It hurt."[32] Bobby Whitley recalled that he and the other guardsmen were "real pissed off" and were drinking beer at the makeshift 'Airport Inn' when Captain Ferrer, whom they highly respected, stopped at the table and said "We don't understand you Anglos. If we get whipped, we quit and fight another day. You Anglos just don't know when to quit."[33]

The dead at the Bay of Pigs included, above left, Wade Gray (courtesy of Joe Shannon); above right, Captain Thomas W. Ray, (courtesy of Southern Museum of Flight); and Leo Baker (courtesy of Southern Museum of Flight).

5

Coping with Death and Defeat

THE CIA WASTED no time closing down operations and pulling out of the secret bases in Guatemala and Nicaragua. Both governments had informed the United States that they wanted the invasion forces out of their countries by June. A handful of Alabamians, Stud Livingston and Ulay Littleton among them, remained at Retalhuleu for a while longer than the other volunteers to help the CIA dispose of equipment and clear the base. The others flew back to Miami in small groups to keep from being conspicuous, and promptly took airline flights home.[1]

The ones who came home were not the same carefree, rowdy bunch who left Birmingham eager to "go south and kick Castro's butt." The younger ones had shed some of their naivete, and had done some growing up. All were depressed by the loss of lifelong friends—in Roy Wilson's case a close family member—and had to shake off feelings of being let down by their own government in its handling of the Bay of Pigs invasion. Buck Persons recalled the C-54 pilot who flew his small group back to Miami saying that if there was a law against hauling drunks, he would get life. The group arrived back in Birmingham slightly hung over, but sober and pensive. Persons passed Leo Baker's pizza shack on the way home, and sadly noticed that "the windows were boarded up."[2]

Not being able to tell the families about what really happened to their loved ones was the hardest part of the guardsmen's return home. Sworn to secrecy for national security reasons, the Air Guard members kept their silence even when a few of the non-guardsmen and the Cuban exiles chose to talk or to write about the Bay of Pigs experience. Word leaked out about the Alabama Guard's role at the Bay of Pigs, but the CIA did not make the operation public or clear the guardsmen to talk about it until more than thirty years after the event. In an interview with Frank Sikora of *The Birmingham News*, Joe Shannon swore that in all that time he had kept the secret even from his wife. In the early 1990s, finally cleared to tell the families of those who were killed at the Bay of Pigs, Shannon sat down with Jane Shamburger and talked with her about her husband Riley's death.[3]

In early May 1961, Shannon and the other guardsmen had to suppress their anger when Miami lawyer Alex E. Carlson showed up in Birmingham with a phony story that the four slain airmen had been hired as mercenaries by a wealthy anti-Castro group and were shot down off the coast of Cuba while flying a C-46 cargo mission. Carlson held a news conference to announce that he was in town to notify the families of the four men who were killed and to arrange insurance payments to the widows. He claimed to represent the Double-Chek Corporation (which was a CIA front), and said the corporation had hired the men for a private group who wished to remain anonymous. The men were presumed to be flying the cargo mission in support of the Bay of Pigs invasion, the Miami lawyer said.[4]

Carlson's public announcement that the slain men were soldiers of fortune did not sit well with their fellow guardsmen or with their widows. An unidentified spokesman for the families angrily denied that the four guardsmen were mercenaries. "They were gallant men,

fighting for the anti-Communist cause they believed in," the spokesman said. Jane Shamburger stated firmly that whatever mission her
husband was engaged in, it was for his country and not for the
money. Riley had served in World War II and Korea, was a major
in the Alabama Air National Guard, and was a top-rated test pilot
for Hayes Aircraft.[5]

The distraught families started putting their lives back together.
Leo Baker's wife Cathy, pregnant with her second child, had to be
hospitalized when she learned he was missing. A native of Boston,
Baker was a Korean War veteran, had been a technical sergeant in
the Air Force and made his home in Birmingham. His daughter
Teresa by a former marriage was twelve years old. He and Cathy had
two children. Beth was one year old, and Mary was born September
26, 1961, six months after her father's death. Wade Gray's wife
Violet resided in the Birmingham suburb of Pinson where her
husband lived most of his life. They had no children. She too
protested that her husband was no soldier of fortune.[6]

At thirty years of age, Thomas "Pete" Ray was the youngest of
the four airmen. He was a Birmingham native and had served in the
Air Force during the Korean War. Ray went to work for Hayes
Aircraft after the war, and he flew B-26s and F-84s with the
Alabama National Guard. He and his wife Margaret had been high
school sweethearts. They had two children, Thomas and Janet, who
were eight and six years old respectively when their father died. The
family moved to Montgomery to start anew, but their lives would
never be the same again.[7]

Unbeknownst to the widowed families at the time, Fidel Castro
had recovered the bodies of Pete Ray and Leo Baker but did not
have their real names. On the day they were killed, Radio Havana
announced that Cuban forces shot down an American bomber and
had recovered the pilots' bodies. The only means of identification
were the false papers the CIA had issued the two men. Since Leo

A retired Alabama Air National Guard RB-26C sits idle in the boneyard at Davis-Monthan AFB, AZ (Photo by Dave Lucabaugh, courtesy of Southern Museum of Flight).

Baker had dark skin and was mistakenly believed to be Latin American, his body was buried in a mass grave with other slain members of the brigade. Ray's body, however, was readily identified as being that of an American, so Castro had the body preserved as evidence to prove the U.S. Government was behind the invasion and to use for propaganda purposes.[8]

Six months after General Doster and the Alabama volunteers returned from the Bay of Pigs operation, the Birmingham unit (the 117th Tactical Reconnaissance Wing) was called to active duty and deployed to Germany during the Berlin Crisis. When the wing redeployed to Birmingham in August 1962 books were being written about the Bay of Pigs and journalists were still raising questions about the deaths of the four Alabama airmen and the Air Guard's involvement. Riley Shamburger's mother wrote to President Kennedy and received a letter back from his Air Force aide, Brigadier General Godfrey T. McHugh, that neither the CIA nor any other government agency possessed information on her son's disappearance. "If any information is ever obtained on the loss of your son you will be informed immediately," the general wrote.[9]

Buck Persons, who became managing editor of the *Birmingham Examiner* after returning from Guatemala, published an article in March 1963 disclosing that the four Alabama airmen were shot down over the Bay of Pigs on April 19, 1961, in a vain effort to stop Castro's forces. Persons agreed to publish the article in *Chicago's American* after one of the paper's reporters contacted him about the role American pilots played in the Cuban invasion. The reporter first got a referral to Reid Doster from another Air Force general, Maj. Gen. David W. Hutchison, a former commander of Ninth Air Force, who told him that Doster was in charge of tactical air operations in the Bay of Pigs. "He'll talk to you if he can," Hutchison said.[10]

When the reporter contacted Doster (who was to put on a second star in November 1963), the general did not refute the alleged remark claiming he had been in charge of air operations in the Cuban invasion but said that he could make no comment. Doster oddly suggested that the reporter contact Buck Persons, who he said was a newspaper editor and claimed to have been one of the pilots supporting the invasion. The reporter called Persons and learned that he had completed one article on the Alabama Guard's role in the Bay of Pigs and was working on a second one. Since an Air Force general had revealed that Doster was involved with the invasion, and Doster had referred the reporter to him, Persons believed this released him from the vow not to talk about the operation. Anyway, he did not belong to the National Guard, and did not feel bound to the same strict rules as the guardsmen.[11]

Before the *Chicago's American* could publish Persons's story, Senator Everett M. Dirksen, Senate minority leader, scooped everyone on February 25, 1963, by revealing the truth about the four Alabama airmen dying in the Bay of Pigs invasion. The disclosure was embarrassing for the White House because Attorney General Robert F. Kennedy had denied in an interview on January 21, 1963, that any Americans died at the Bay of Pigs. The attorney general admitted on the record, for the first time, that the CIA was responsible for the invasion and that President Kennedy and the Joint Chiefs had approved it.[12]

In the story carried by the *Chicago's American* on March 7, Persons emphasized that the American pilots and crews who were involved with the Bay of Pigs invasion "were not irresponsible adventurers." They had volunteered for the mission at the request of the U.S. Government. Persons, whose writings reflected the feelings of betrayal shared by many of the guardsmen, described those who served:

> All were mature, experienced pilots and aircrewmen. All were married. All had families . . . and good jobs. Each was motivated by something more than a paycheck. By some standards we were well paid. Any of us would have accepted the job for nothing if asked.[13]

Persons's article placed the blame squarely on President Kennedy and the constraints he placed on air operations for the failure of the invasion. He also defended the CIA's handling of the invasion and decried the "deliberate and unwarranted abuse" heaped on the Agency after it failed. He praised the CIA for keeping its silence when "heads rolled" at the headquarters. "I'm a little surprised however, that most of the American people seem to accept the criticism of the CIA as justified," Persons wrote.[14]

On March 6, at a Presidential press conference, a journalist asked whether the four Americans who died in the Bay of Pigs invasion were employees of the government or the CIA. President Kennedy answered: "They were serving their country. The flight that cost them their lives was a volunteer flight, and that while

Captain Ferrer and Admiral Arleigh Burke in 1978. The two men became friends after the Bay of Pigs and visited together frequently. Admiral Burke had urged President Kennedy to unleash jet fighters from the carrier Essex against Castro's forces at the Bay of Pigs, but to no avail (courtesy of Captain Ferrer).

because of the nature of their work it has not been a matter of public record, as it might be in the case of soldiers or sailors, I can say they were serving their country . . . ."[15]

BUCK PERSONS'S BITTERNESS toward the Kennedy Administration resulted from his deep-seated belief, shared by many of his comrades who supported the Cuban invasion, that the administration had betrayed them and then used the CIA as a scapegoat to cover up White House mistakes. Recriminations had flown left and right in the wake of the failed invasion. President Kennedy accepted full blame for the outcome, then "asked for the resignations of CIA Director Allen Dulles and Richard Bissell, the spymaster who had directed the invasion."[16] On the day after the invasion, in an address before the American Society of Newspaper Editors, Kennedy said again that "unilateral American intervention in Cuba would have been contrary to traditions and international obligations," but warned that "our restraint is not inexhaustible."[17]

The mood in Washington was gray, but there was a determination to continue the fight against Castro. Kennedy stated that the United States still supported Cuban freedom fighters who were aligned against Castro and were determined not to abandon Cuba to the communists. "The Cuban people have not yet spoken their final piece—and I have no doubt that they will continue to speak up for a free and independent Cuba," Kennedy said.[18]

The President was not only disappointed in the advice he got from the CIA, but in the opinions from the Joint Chiefs of Staff as well. It was customary that there be a changing of the guard when a new chief executive moved into the White House, so it was time for a change at the Pentagon anyway. Kennedy had already appointed Robert S. McNamara, whose high-handed business style clashed with the military way of doing things, as Secretary of Defense. He now called on General Maxwell D. Taylor, former Army chief of staff, to advise him on military matters and had him lead an inquiry into the Bay of Pigs failure.

The Taylor Board tied the failure directly to the lack of success in destroying Castro's aircraft on the ground, which allowed his T-33s to sink the resupply ships. An internal survey by the CIA's inspector general, Lyman Kirkpatrick, was highly critical of the way the agency planned and conducted the Cuban operation. The Kirkpatrick report, which Richard Bissell said "was more ruthless in its conclusions and caused an uproar at the agency, especially with Dulles and Cabell," remained classified and was not released to the public until 1997. The conclusions, which appear to be anticlimactic at the end of nearly forty years, make it clear that the CIA should

have made a stronger case to the White House that everything
hinged on destroying Castro's aircraft, that the invasion could not
succeed without control of the air.[19]

Neither McNamara nor the Joint Chiefs of Staff were of much
help to the White House in making decisions on the Cuban
invasion. As JCS position papers would later reveal during the
Vietnam War, the system often forced military chiefs into promot-
ing individual service interests and providing decision makers with
more options than solid military guidance for making the right "go-
no-go" decisions. In planning and carrying out the Cuban invasion,
Admiral Arleigh Burke was the one member of the JCS who spoke
unequivocally to the President about needing greater air strength,
including intervention by carrier aircraft if necessary, to deny
Castro a victory at the Bay of Pigs.

Admiral Burke later confided in Captain Edward Ferrer, who
became friends with the admiral after the failed invasion, that he
and the other JCS members had protested the president's decision
to reduce the initial air strikes, but could not change his mind.
Burke said he personally warned the president that "if Castro were
left with only one fighter plane, it would be enough to destroy the
invaders' ships and planes." There were two aircraft carriers among
the fleet of U.S. warships the president had authorized Admiral
Burke to dispatch to international waters near the Bay of Pigs. On
board the carrier *Essex* was a dozen A4-D fighters with the Navy
insignias removed, while 2,000 Marines waiting aboard a transport
ship were ready to go into battle if ordered ashore.[20]

On the second day of the invasion when the brigade's situation
looked hopeless, Admiral Burke urged the president to authorize
the *Essex* to launch its A4Ds to shoot down the enemy planes. When
Kennedy denied the request, Burke asked that the U.S. destroyers
be allowed to fire on Castro's advancing tanks. Kennedy repeated
that he did not want U.S. forces involved. "Goddamn, Mr. Presi-

dent," Burke is said to have argued. "We are already involved and there is nothing you can do about it." There is irony in the fact that when the president did authorize the A4Ds to provide air cover the following morning, the mission was not carried out because the U.S. Navy and the CIA could not get their times straight.[21]

President Kennedy had approved positioning the U.S. Navy ships in the area only to defend the small invasion fleet in case it was discovered and attacked in international waters. The ships were not there to support the invasion. Without U.S. air support, some critics argued that the 16 light bombers and small pilot force were grossly inadequate for the job. Military analysts for *Time* bluntly accused U.S. planners, including the Joint Chiefs of Staff, of incompetence for relying on only 16 B-26s for air cover. "They knew that Castro had a force of T-33s, and they also knew that after the long flight from Puerto Cabezas the B-26s would have only enough fuel left to keep aloft for forty minutes over the target area," *Time* stated.[22] The analysts neglected to mention that the planners were limited to the number and type of aircraft used and their operating location by political not doctrinal considerations, i.e. the need to mask the U.S. Government's involvement in the affair.

Every post-invasion analysis of the operation pointed to the failure to destroy Castro's aircraft as a primary factor in the brigade's defeat. Even Fidel Castro was quoted as saying that the Cuban exiles had failed because "they had no air support." Arthur Schlesinger said that Kennedy came later to feel that cancelling the second air strike was a mistake, but did not regard the decision to cancel the air strikes as decisive. While admitting that the second strike might have protracted the stand on the beachhead for a few days, Schlesinger concluded that without U.S. intervention, which was never an option, it would not have reversed the outcome.[23]

Schlesinger's argument missed the point, as far as the Cuban freedom fighters and their American advisers were concerned.

Destroying Castro's aircraft at the outset would have saved lives, including those of American and Cuban pilots, and would have helped even the odds—giving the brigade a fighting chance against the far superior numbers of Castro's ground forces. At least of equal weight was the decision to change the landing site from the Trinidad area where the brigade theoretically had a better chance of winning local support or escaping to the mountains if they had to.

At the heart of the problem was an evolving pattern for micromanaging military operations, or in this case paramilitary operations, from the White House. This pattern cast a long shadow over budding military actions in Southeast Asia and much further down the road during the abortive attempt to free American hostages in Iran. There were other lessons unlearned from the Bay of Pigs debacle. The misreading of intelligence reports, which resulted in underestimating Castro's military capabilities and overestimating the prospects for a popular uprising, would be repeated tenfold in the Vietnam War. The arrogance that the CIA showed in such things as planning the invasion without input from the Cuban brigade manifested itself time and again in Vietnam. In *Operation Puma*, Captain Ferrer pointed to this incongruity. "Had they ever considered that as Cubans about to invade Cuba, we would be able to provide some valuable input, pertaining to geography and the state of mind of the Cuban people, which might be a factor in their planning?" he asked.[24]

Questions about the cancelled air strikes would not go away. In his memoirs Bissell told about renewing contact with John McCone (who succeeded Allen Dulles as CIA director) in 1985 and being asked for his version of the discussions leading to Kennedy's decision to call off the air strikes. "It was this fatal error that caused the failure of the Bay of Pigs operation," McCone stated.[25] Colonel Jack Hawkins agreed and, in an article published in *Military History* nearly four decades after the attempted invasion, placed the blame directly at the feet of Richard Bissell and General Charles Cabell for not "falling on their swords" with the President over the cancelled airstrikes.[26]

Colonel Hawkins noted that recently declassified papers revealed that Bissell had agreed at least three days before the pre-invasion airstrikes to reduce the number of bombers by half. He had not informed Esterline and Hawkins until one day before the strikes, which was too late to have the decision reversed. It had been only a few days since Esterline and Hawkins had gone to Bissell's home to express their opposition to going ahead with the invasion. Hawkins believed that Bissell, by not heeding their advice, had pushed "a reluctant president into a foolhardy and hopeless military venture. . . . The result was a major foreign policy debacle, which led to the establishment of a threatening military presence in Cuba, the Cuban missile crisis and the brink of nuclear war," he concluded.[27]

THE CUBAN PROBLEM HAUNTED John F. Kennedy's presidency. Fidel Castro's swift victory at the Bay of Pigs strengthened his hold on government power, added greatly to his stature among communist bloc nations and Third World leaders, and boosted his popularity with the Cuban people. Despite all the precautions, the U.S. Government could not hide its complicity in the invasion. The week after the debacle *Time* reported that "the U.S. had done everything to assure success short of providing an air cover or sending in the Marines. . . . The invaders—all Cubans—were trained by the U.S., supplied by the U.S., and dispatched by the U.S. to carry out a plan written by U.S. military experts."[28]

The worldwide reaction was "loud and predictable." A *Life* staff writer described the "worldwide jeers" that were directed toward the United States for the "hell of a beating" that it took at the Bay of Pigs. Even staunch allies "openly showed both scorn and dismay at U.S. bungling." The *Life* staffer wrote:

Nikita Khrushchev accused President Kennedy of "gangster-ism." In Communist capitals student mobs dutifully chimed in, letting fly at U.S. embassies with sticks, stones and outrageous charges. Here and there in Latin America, pro Castro forces ran riots—a number of them bloody—against "Yankee imperial-ism."[29]

Castro played the episode for all it was worth. *Time* reported that "the Castro regime's triumphant cock's crow of victory, for all of its exaggerations, was close to the bitter truth." The weekly magazine painted a vivid description of the "Roman Circus" atmo-sphere in Havana as Cubans prepared to "celebrate the defeat of the 'North American mercenaries' with the greatest parade in history":

> On Havana street corners, groups of prancing militiamen fired their Czech burp guns into the air and Jeeps draped with hot-eyed youths careened along the avenues. Communist-country corre-spondents were hustled off to the shell-pocked beachhead to view the wreckage of invasion—U.S.-made mortars, recoilless rifles, trucks, machine guns, rifles, and medium tanks. A few of the captured survivors were shown on TV, while commentators jabbed jubilant questions at them.[30]

When one of the commentators asked a twenty-nine-year-old parachutist, who admitted to having been misled to believe the brigade would be welcomed by the Cuban people, what he now thought about the Cuban Revolution, the prisoner wryly replied, "Well, maybe I'll be here long enough to form an opinion." At a mass trial ordered by Castro each of the Bay of Pigs captives was sentenced to thirty years in prison, but the wily dictator sought to ransom the prisoners by offering to free them for repayment of damages the United States had inflicted on the Cuban people.[31]

In May 1961 Castro offered to exchange the prisoners for tractors and agricultural machinery. At President Kennedy's request, Mrs. Eleanor Roosevelt, Dr. Milton S. Eisenhower, and Walter Reuther formed a "Tractors for Freedom" Committee to collect funds from private donors for negotiating the release of the prisoners. Castro formed a commission made up of ten brigade prisoners to negotiate with the committee. Negotiations broke down after the proposed exchange of tractors for prisoners came under harsh criticism from partisan members of Congress.[32]

In April 1962, as Havana celebrated the first anniversary of its victory at the Bay of Pigs, Fidel Castro released sixty of the most seriously wounded prisoners so they could return to the United States and help raise funds to buy the release of their comrades. The return of the sixty prisoners was negotiated by the Cuban Families Committee, an organization formed by Alvaro Sanchez, Jr., and represented by lawyer James Donovan. Seven months later, in November 1962, Attorney General Robert Kennedy met with Sanchez and Donovan at the Waldorf-Astoria Hotel in New York and gave the government's approval to negotiate for release of the prisoners in exchange for $53 million worth of food and medicine donated by private firms. Castro agreed to the exchange, with the understanding that it be completed by Christmas 1962.[33]

For eighteen months the invasion prisoners had been crowded into cells and left to waste away. Once the agreement was made in late November, the prisoners stated that Castro "started to fatten them up" saying he did not want them "looking like a lot of bums." They were issued new clothing to replace the tattered remnants of the uniforms they had worn at the Bay of Pigs. "Castro's 'generosity' served its purpose," according to *U.S. News & World Report*. "It was a handsome group—clean-shaven and newly clothed—that stepped off planes in Miami at Christmas time." James Donovan also persuaded Castro to let more than 900 of their relatives leave Cuba for the United States.[34] Castro reportedly used the ransom money to pay off his debts to eastern European countries for military assistance and food shipments.

While working to free the brigade members captured at the Bay of Pigs, Donovan seized the opportunity to try and win freedom for twenty-one Americans still locked away in Cuban prisons. Among the American prisoners was Tommy L. Baker, a thirty-year-old Dothan, Alabama, man whose death sentence by military court in January 1961 had been commuted to thirty years imprisonment. Baker was captured with five other American adventurers aboard a Florida-based yacht and was charged with attempting to smuggle guns to anti-Castro guerrillas.[35]

Cuban police charged that the six Americans had attempted to land on the north coast of Pinar Del Rio Province, a rebel stronghold, but bad weather forced them to sail into Havana harbor. The men reportedly dumped their weapons and equipment overboard before landing. In letters home that were smuggled out of Cuba by Frank Beatty, a photographer for United Press International who was released from a Cuban prison in January 1961, Tommy Baker expressed fear that he might "be sent to the wall and shot." More than 600 persons, including several American citizens, had been put to death by firing squad since Castro took over the government in 1958.[36]

There was a ray of hope in the fact that the Cuban court had commuted the death sentences of Baker and his companions. Alabama Governor John Patterson, when interviewed by *The Birmingham News*, said the verdict still seemed "pretty tough" to him. He had hoped the Castro regime would let the men off as a good will gesture to the new administration of John F. Kennedy. The governor joined in appeals to U.S. Government officials for intervention with Cuban authorities in behalf of Baker and his companions.[37]

Captain Ferrer salutes President Kennedy inside the Orange Bowl in Miami in January 1963 after Castro released the prisoners captured at the Bay of Pigs in exchange for food and medicine (courtesy of Captain Ferrer).

Any hopes of getting the six Americans released were lost in the harsh rhetoric coming out of Cuba in the aftermath of the Bay of Pigs invasion. Not until after the ransom of the Cuban exiles in December 1962 were conditions right for New York Attorney James Donovan to begin negotiating for the release of the American prisoners. In March 1963 Donovan wrote Tommy Baker's parents in Dothan that he had visited their son at the Isle of Pines Prison and that he was in good health and "in reasonably good spirits." The attorney had negotiated for the release of the prisoners, but Castro presumably was waiting until the last ransom ship of medicine and goods arrived at the Havana harbor before letting them go.[38]

On April 22 Donovan flew with the six Americans to Home-stead AFB, Florida, where they were reunited with their families. A banquet was held for the men in a Miami hotel, which served the guests "tender, savory beefsteak." The men had told their families "how they used to catch cats in a Castro prison and eat them to appease their hunger." In Washington, D.C., Attorney General Robert Kennedy announced that the Americans were released in a prisoner exchange for four Cubans (three alleged saboteurs and a convicted murderer) who were being held in the United States.[39]

Earlier, after the return of the Cuban exiles, the President and First Lady received the brigade leaders at their Palm Beach home. Afterward the President addressed the brigade members and friends at the Orange Bowl. He pledged that the brigade's flag would someday fly "in a free Havana." Nearly a year before getting the prisoners released, the President approved a new, more ambitious paramilitary program against Castro called Operation Mongoose. His brother Bobby and General Maxwell Taylor took an active interest in Mongoose, and the Air Force's near-legendary Brigadier General Edward Lansdale was assigned as executive officer for the operation. President Kennedy was determined to bring Castro down, and might have succeeded if not for the sniper's bullet in Dallas on November 22, 1963.[40] Unfortunately, the bearded dicta-tor survived Camelot to become a thorn in the side of eight successive U.S. presidents.

106th Tactical Reconnaissance Squadron, Alabama Air National Guard, after the Bay of Pigs. (Sitting, L to R) Bill Fultz, Gary Ellis, Walter Blake, Warren Brown, Zymer Ingram, Devand Hammond, Jack Phillips. (Kneeling, L to R) Captain Bill Baker, Danny Morris, Hoyt Carroll, Wiley Johnson, John O. Spinks, George Holbrooks, William Bennifield, Bobby Newsome, Glenn Fraley, Jack Mohon, Mac Hickman, George Dibbeman, Clifford Hayes, Louis Hudson, James Glenn. (Standing, L to R) Joe Fancher, Edward Gober, Max Campbell, Bill Sizemore, Kenneth Owens, Don Chandler, Virgil Sanders, Fred Raley, Robert Stanley, Donald Crocker, Johnny Burton, Harold Black, Curtiss Farley, Johnny Singleton, Milton Padgett, Bill Estoch, Albert Cordes, Glenn Harris, George Ouslin, Walter Carroll, Tom Rowan, Will Franklin, E.P. Green, (On Aircraft, L to R) Capt. Charles Crow, Preston Myers, Charles Welch, Joel Kilgore, Carr Scott, Bobby Weeks, Bobby Whitley, Ted Campbell.

6

The Survivors

FORMER ALABAMA Air National Guard members who are veterans of the Bay of Pigs operation and are still living have mellowed over the past forty years. They know in their hearts that what they did to support the Cuban invasion was the right thing to do and, with perhaps a few exceptions, still believe strongly that had the President not changed the original plans calling for landing on the beaches near the populous city of Trinidad and for performing sustained air attacks to knock out Castro's air forces, there would have been a different outcome. They say this matter-of-factly, not with rancor or bitterness. Although wearing mufti while working for the CIA in Guatemala and Nicaragua, the guardsmen were military men through and through. They did their jobs and returned to Birmingham ready for their next mission, whenever and wherever the orders read.

James Harrison was one guardsman who questioned whether the invasion could have been successful without the use of U.S. military power. He hastened to add that he never expected U.S. troops to be used, although this might have been "wishful thinking" on the part of some who were involved. Harrison said that when the pilots got back and discussed the situation among themselves, they agreed that air support for the invasion "was a very poorly organized and planned operation." He elaborated:

> The personnel selectivity was bad. We were not well enough trained to do the job. We did not have the proper equipment nor the proper aircraft to do the job. It was very loosely organized. Too loose. No one knew who their boss or the boss was. It was a terrible, a horrible thing to be involved. I am sorry I was part of the mission because we were not prepared and didn't have the right equipment for the job.[1]

The guardsmen were home only six months when President Kennedy mobilized twenty-nine Air National Guard squadrons, including the Birmingham unit, in response to the Berlin Crisis. At a summit meeting with President Kennedy in June, Soviet Premier Nikita Khrushchev—apparently emboldened by Kennedy's indecisiveness on the Cuban invasion—raised the specter of war in Europe by threatening to sign a separate treaty with East Berlin. When the Soviet Union escalated the crisis by dividing the city with roadblocks and barricades and starting construction of the Berlin Wall, Kennedy called Khrushchev's bluff by building up conventional military power in NATO Europe.[2]

Birmingham guardsmen, as part of this buildup, were deployed to Europe for several months until the crisis was over. Unlike the secrecy surrounding the Alabama Guard's role at the Bay of Pigs, the deployment to Europe under Operation Stair Step was a highly publicized show of force. The Alabama Air Guard and its high-profile leader Reid Doster were publicly praised for their part in the East-West staredown. General Doster made his second star in November 1963 and was appointed commander of the Alabama Air National Guard in June 1966. He had become a highly visible public figure around the state. Whether the blustery general har-

Major General Doster greeted by the 17th Air Force Commander on arriving at Ramstein Air Base, Germany, during the Berlin Crisis (ANG Photo).

bored political ambitions is not known, but according to ace reporter Dave Langford, Doster was "up to his bushy eyebrows in Alabama politics—a hobby that eventually would cost him his job."[3]

Langford noted that Doster was not circumspect in some of his political dealings. The general made no pretense of hiding the sumptuous parties he threw for state officials at Guard expense, openly boasting about flying in 700 lobsters for a single event. In January 1965 Doster made headlines again when Attorney General Richmond Flowers opened a full-scale investigation into charges that Air Guard planes had transported some 44 cases of non-taxed "brand name" liquors into Alabama illegally with General Doster's approval. The illegal cases of liquor were brought in from out of state for a private party in Birmingham. The alleged flight occurred during the middle of a boycott of Alabama by major distilleries protesting a newly imposed three percent state sales tax. Doster contended that the flight did not violate state laws since the Air Guard facility in Birmingham was a Federal base. Governor George Wallace, seeing things differently, ordered Doster's boss Adjutant General Alfred Harrison to see that no more liquor was transported in the state's National Guard planes.[4]

Two months later, in March 1965, a $100,000 slander and libel suit was filed against Doster in connection with the case. Lieutenant Colonel David Whiteside, commander of the Alabama Guard's 117th Tactical Reconnaissance Group, filed the suit claiming that Doster gave "slanderous information" to a Birmingham radio station and United Press International, accusing a "disgruntled lieutenant colonel" of bringing to light the alleged purchase and transport of non-taxed liquor. Whiteside, who said he had no part in the flight or the purchase, charged that he had resigned from his Birmingham post because of "wrongful and malicious interference" with his duties as group commander.[5]

The illegal whiskey and libel cases did not cost Doster his job, but they were embarrassing for both the general and the Alabama Guard. Several years later, in February 1972, the two-star general faced more serious charges when a federal grand jury indicted him and three subordinates for violating the Hatch Act by conspiring to solicit political contributions from fellow officers during the 1970 governor's race. The indictment charged the four officers with raising $1,700 for Governor George C. Wallace's successful campaign in the Democratic primary and $1,000 for Albert Brewer, a Wallace opponent who was governor at the time. The investigation leading to the indictments began when an Air Guard major complained that he had been harassed and threatened for refusing to contribute to the campaign funds.[6]

Adjutant General Charles A. Rollo, whose office oversaw the Alabama Guard, fired Doster and the other officers but later recommended fines instead of dismissal for all except Doster. The U.S. Civil Service Commission set aside the discharge, however, and suspended him instead for 120 days pending trial. After U.S. District Judge Frank M. Johnson denied a motion for a change of venue from Montgomery to Birmingham, the trial was set for Monday, August 21, 1972, with District Judge Robert Varner presiding.[7]

Minutes before the trial was scheduled to begin, U.S. Attorney Ira DeMent announced in federal court that an agreement had been reached whereby he would dismiss cases against all four officers after Doster relinquished his commission as major general, his assignment as state Air Guard chief of staff and his civilian job as detachment commander of Sumpter Smith Air National Guard Base in Birmingham. Judge Varner granted a continuance of the cases until November 3, when the threefold resignation by Doster became effective. The fifty-four-year-old Doster retained his U.S. Air Force reserve status as a major general and his eligibility for

(L to R) Connie Seigrith, his son, Douglas R. Price, and Carl Sudano at 1989 reunion. CIA pilots Seigrith and Price flew B-26 combat missions on the second day of the Bay of Pigs invasion (courtesy of Carl Sudano).

retirement benefits from the Air Guard and civil service when he reached retirement age.[8]

The U.S. Attorney, Ira DeMent, revealed recently that the CIA had interceded on Doster's behalf because of his active support during the Bay of Pigs invasion. "The CIA called the Attorney General's office and they called me," DeMent stated. "The Attorney General asked me if I would dismiss the indictment if Doster resigned his Air National Guard commission. Of course I said yes. He resigned and the charges were dropped."[9]

The charismatic two-star general opened his own business in Birmingham after resigning in November 1972 according to the terms of the plea agreement. Doster remained popular among many of his former subordinates, but one veteran guardsmen recalled bitterly that, "there was a lot of rotten stuff going on in the Guard

(L to R) Roy Wilson, James Vaughn, Joe Shannon, Carl Sudano, and Joel Kilgore at the Bay of Pigs memorial in Havana during a 1989 reunion. Vaughn was a CIA civilian who flew with Billy "Dodo" Goodwin on the final day of the invasion (courtesy of Carl Sudano).

after the Bay of Pigs." He personally believed that Doster "was not real general officer material" and "was not man enough for the job." Before his death in the 1990s Doster spoke freely with reporters about his experience with the Bay of Pigs and about the political shenanigans that eventually got him in trouble.[10]

Lieutenant Colonel Joe Shannon is the sole surviving Air Guard pilot who flew on the perilous B-26 mission over the Bay of Pigs on 19 April. Major Billy "Dodo" Goodwin, the only other Guard pilot to survive the mission, has since died. Joe Shannon retired from the Alabama Guard in November 1972, and is also a retired commercial pilot. Having flown everything from the RAF's Supermarine Spitfire to the McDonnell RF-4C Phantom II, Shannon has devoted his life to military aviation. He celebrated his 80th birthday, as the 40th Anniversary of the Bay of Pigs approached in April

2001. Shannon is on the board of directors for the Southern Museum of Flight in Birmingham, and was recently inducted into the Alabama Aviation Hall of Fame.[11]

Carl Sudano, who accompanied Shannon on the B-26 mission, now lives in Palm Beach Gardens, Florida. The two men have stayed in close touch since the Bay of Pigs. "Joe is one of my best friends," Sudano told an interviewer recently. The Bay of Pigs was not Sudano's only connection to the CIA. He later worked with the Agency for about five years maintaining B-26s that were operating in Laos. He also worked for Grumman Aircraft Corporation for twenty years. Since moving to Florida, the former Alabama guardsman has become reacquainted with the Cuban friends he served with at Puerto Cabezas. He still attends the Bay of Pigs reunion in Miami each year.[12]

Shannon and Sudano were recognized for their heroic mission at the Bay of Pigs during a special ceremony in Birmingham on January 20, 2001. CIA officials presented agency seal medallions to Shannon and Sudano, and to family members of two deceased Air Guard Pilots, Billy Goodwin and Dalton Livingston. A fifth medallion was reserved for the family of James W. Vaughn, a deceased CIA employee from Birmingham who flew with Goodwin at the Bay of Pigs. Leading the CIA delegation was the agency's associate military director, Lieutenant General John H. Campbell, who told the Alabama guardsmen and family members that their service and their sacrifice would not be forgotten.[13]

At a military banquet hosted by the Air Guard wing in Birmingham on May 13, 2000, only 16 veterans of the Bay of Pigs operation were in attendance. In addition to Joe Shannon the attendees were William D. Bainbridge, William P. Baker, Willie E. Colvert, Donald R. Crocker, Joseph A. Fancher, William C. Fultz, James C. Glenn, William R. Gray, James W. Harrison, Louis H. Hudson, John O. Spinks, Robert L. Stanley, Bobby A. Whitley, Roy H.

Carl Sudano (L) and Joe Shannon (R) during award of the 2506
Assault Brigade's Medal for Valor (courtesy of Carl Sudano).

Wilson, and Charles R. Yates. During the banquet Wing commander Kirk J. Tyree presided over a ceremony honoring their
participation in the Bay of Pigs operation. A plaque bearing their
names and those of their comrades will be permanently displayed at
the 117th Wing in their honor.[14]

Many of the Alabama Guard veterans of the Bay of Pigs
operation are deceased. Others have moved away and were unavail-
able for the reunion. All are retired now, but their lives are still
dedicated to the support of their country and military readiness.
Only the spring has gone out of their step, not the sparkle from their
eyes. They still enjoy good mischief and are as full of vinegar as the
day they volunteered to go and help the CIA and the exiled patriots
fight for a free Cuba. Sometimes they drive by the Airport Inn and
there is a lump in their throat, but they don't stop there anymore.

The tables full of empties, the jukebox blaring with a country
song, and the raucous laughter of the Airport Inn are for the
younger guys who now climb down from the cockpit or who keep
flightline maintenance humming. The ghosts of the fifties and
sixties are still alive in these young airmen. They too will go where
duty calls, anyplace and anytime. As Birmingham newspaperman
Thomas Bailey was quoted as saying when asked what made his
cousin Pete Ray volunteer to fly the mission that ended in his death
at the Bay of Pigs: "We all grew up Southern, patriotic, independent
and ornery. We grew up scrapping and fighting, saying this is my
country, by God, and don't mess with it."[15]

OF THE FOUR ALABAMA GUARDSMEN killed at the Bay of Pigs,
Thomas Ray's body is the only one to date that has been recovered
and returned home for burial. Ray's son Thomas and daughter
Janet were small children when their father died. They never gave
up on finding the truth about his death and bringing him home.
Their persistence finally paid off in September 1979 when the FBI

officially identified a corpse that had been refrigerated in a Havana morgue for seventeen years as Thomas Ray's body. In December 1979 the U.S. Government arranged to bring Ray's body home where he was given a military funeral and laid to rest on a Birmingham hillside.[16]

Janet now resides in Miami with her husband Mike Weininger, a pilot for Delta Airlines and an F-16 pilot in the Air Force Reserve, and their two children. Her brother Tom is an attorney residing in California. A couple of years before the FBI identified her father's body, Janet learned that the Havana morgue had the refrigerated body of an American pilot killed at the Bay of Pigs. Fidel Castro had mentioned the corpse during a visit to Cuba by U.S. officials. The corpse had been preserved as proof of "Yankee aggression" against Cuba.[17]

Janet was not living in Miami at the time she and her brother learned that their father's body might be in the Havana morgue. They made numerous trips to the city to talk with veterans of Brigade 2506 about their father's death. Convinced that it was her father's body in the Havana morgue, Janet pressed U.S. Government officials to have the body officially identified and returned home for burial. U.S. Representative John Buchanan, a Baptist minister from Birmingham, took an interest in the case and helped persuade U.S. and Cuban officials to cooperate in returning the body to the United States. FBI officials were sent to Cuba and identified Ray's body by matching it with fingerprints and dental records. [18]

In 1978, while Thomas Ray's family lobbied to have his body returned, the CIA finally told the families of the Alabama guardsmen who were killed at the Bay of Pigs the truth about what happened to them. At the same time the CIA posthumously awarded the four Alabama Guard heroes the Distinguished Intelligence Cross, the Agency's highest medal for bravery. The officials presenting the medals asked the families not to reveal how their loved ones died to anyone else. Even after Ray's body was returned to Birmingham for burial, the CIA's strict security regulations precluded acknowledging publicly that the deceased guardsmen were serving their country when they were killed. It was another two decades before the information could be officially released to the public.[19]

In May 1997 the families of the slain Alabama guardsmen were invited to CIA headquarters in Langley, Virginia, for a ceremony honoring seventy agency personnel who gave their lives in the service of their country. In the cavernous lobby of the headquarters the families were guests at the unveiling of the CIA's Wall of Honor, described by *The Washington Post* as "a field of black stars chiseled into a sheer white face of Vermont marble, flanked on the left by the American flag and on the right by the agency's banner." Encased in front of the wall was the Book of Honor, within which all but 29 stars were nameless. Following a thirty-minute ceremony, "taps resounded through the marble foyer" and the families attended a brief reception before leaving the headquarters. Vividly described in *The Washington Post* were "the twin burdens of grief and secrecy" borne by the families:

> Even in Washington, a city of monuments, the CIA's Wall of Honor stands apart. The FBI, the State Department, and even Amtrak have their own memorial walls listing officers and employees who died in the line of duty. The lowliest grunt has his place of honor on the Vietnam wall. Only the CIA remembers its dead with nameless stars. If the CIA's wall is a memorial to the agency's martyrs, it is also a monument to its culture of secrecy.[20]

Included among the names in the Book of Honor were those of the four Alabama guardsmen killed at the Bay of Pigs. Thomas Ray and Leo Baker reportedly survived the crash of their B-26 only to be killed on the ground by Castro's militia. Divergent stories have appeared about what happened after Ray and Baker left the cockpit. A television documentary filmed in 1999 features a dramatic reenactment of Ray dying in a running gun battle with Cuban soldiers. Journalists for the *Los Angeles Times* interviewed a Cuban general who said witnesses saw Ray and Baker flee their downed plane and run into a nearby cane field. Soldiers who tracked the men down and killed them claimed they were acting in self-defense. Birmingham Coroner Jay M. Glass who examined Thomas Ray's corpse determined that Ray had been shot six times, once in the head at close range. He concluded that the shot to the head was a coup de grace and that Ray had been executed.[21]

The return of Thomas Ray's body in December 1979 gave Catherine Baker reason to hope that her husband's body might also be found and brought back to the United States for burial. In 1982, however, the State Department informed her that Leo Baker's body had been dumped into a common grave with other corpses from the Bay of Pigs battle in the Cristobel Colon cemetery of Havana. Apparently Baker, because of his Latin features, was believed to be one of the Cuban exiles. According to the Cuban authorities Baker's body could not be returned to the United States because it was impossible to separate the remains buried in the common grave.[22]

It is unlikely that the bodies of Riley Shamburger and Wade Gray will ever be recovered and returned to the United States, since their plane crashed into the sea somewhere off the coast of Cuba. This may not be the case, however, if Janet Ray Weininger has anything to say about it. Janet has shown great compassion and perseverance not only in efforts to identify her own father's body and to bring him home, but in helping other families find closure in the death of their loved ones. After eighteen years of looking for her father, Janet told herself that if anyone else was in the same situation she was going to help them. "I'm a firm believer that when someone has given his life serving his country you must return those remains to the country," she said.[23]

Even before moving to Miami, Janet had become well-known in the exile community of Little Havana where she had often come as a young girl seeking information about her father. They liked Janet and admired her for all that she had done to keep her father's memory alive and to bring his remains back from Cuba. It was not surprising that the families of two Cuban exiles whose crippled B-26 had crashed into the coastal jungle of Nicaragua during the Bay of Pigs invasion came to Janet for help in locating the crash site and recovering the missing bodies. The missing men were pilot Crispin Garcia and his copilot Juan de Mata Gonzalez, two of ten crewmen who lost their lives during the costly air battle on April 17, 1961, the first day of the Cuban invasion.[24]

Several months after the failed invasion the CIA found the wreckage, which contained three bodies instead of two. The third body was believed to be a stowaway, but could not be explained and has never been identified. At the suggestion of Cuban exile political leader Miro Cardona, the CIA left the bodies at the crash site where local peasants had buried them. There was concern that returning the remains would provide fodder for Castro's propaganda machine and could be politically embarrassing to the U.S. and Nicaraguan governments. Thirty-four years later, when the CIA refused to reveal the location of the crash site, Janet was determined to help the family find the place herself. In 1995 she flew with a small party including Crispin Garcia's son, Frank Garcia, to Nicaragua where a former Nicaraguan Contra fighter agreed to guide them to the site of the crash. Traveling by mule, they reached the site near the remote village of San Jose de Bocay after trekking four hours through the jungle. They found the wreckage, but no bodies.[25]

Before leaving Nicaragua Janet received promises of help from the U.S. Embassy in Managua and the Nicaraguan government of President Arnoldo Aleman Lacayo. Returning home she went to Washington to plead her case in person with the CIA. In 1997 the CIA agreed to assist her and arranged for a team from the Army's Central Identification Laboratory in Hawaii to go to Nicaragua with four Blackhawk helicopters to dig up the remains. Janet went back to Nicaragua in March 1998 to accompany the Army team to the crash site. After a month of painstaking work the team recovered the remains and returned them to the United States for DNA testing. After a year of testing the remains were positively identified as those of the two Cuban heroes and, with Janet's help the remains were flown to Miami for burial.[26]

On Veterans Day, November 11, 2000, Crispin Garcia and Juan Gonzalez were buried in Miami with full military honors from the Cuban American Veterans Association. Reverend Sergio Carrillo, a Bay of Pigs paratrooper, presided over the ceremony. The families hoped someday to take the remains home to a free Cuba. Frank Garcia recalled a letter he received from his father just before his fifth birthday. In the letter, Crispin Garcia promised his son a birthday gift soon when "you return to Cuba and are able to think freely without fear of repression, when you will be able to be with your grandparents and see that in Cuba there is liberty. That will be my gift to you, a free homeland."[27]

During Janet Weininger's trips to Nicaragua she had been deeply touched by the plight of the people she met in San Jose de Bocay and other remote jungle villages. The people, living in abject poverty, had been forgotten because of the remoteness and harsh terrain, the lack of education and the means to communicate, and the dangerous mines left behind from the guerrilla war in Nicaragua. She had grown close to Siete Mares, a former Nicaraguan resistance commander who had assisted her since 1995, and the local villagers who had accepted her as one of them. Her compassion

(Front row, L to R) Bob Whitley, Clarence Sullivan, Bill Fultz (holding CIA seal), Carl N. Sudano, Joseph L. Shannon, Roy Wilson, Don Crocker, and Fred Raley. (Second row, L to R) Bill Gray, Bill Bainbridge, unidentified, Bob Scoggins, and Lou Hudson at CIA award ceremony on January 20, 2001 (courtesy of Dr. Ed Stevenson).

Carl "Nick" Sudano with a restored B-26 Douglas Invader at the Bay of Pigs Memorial in Miami in the background. Sudano flew with Joe Shannon on the final day of the Bay of Pigs invasion (courtesy of Carl Sudano).

led Janet to found Wings of Valor, Inc., a humanitarian organization dedicated to rebuilding lives torn apart by war, poverty and disaster.[28]

When Hurricane Mitch devastated Central America in 1998, thousands of people were killed or missing, and millions were left homeless with their houses and harvests destroyed beyond recovery. Janet led a drive to obtain private donations and Delta Airlines provided a Good Samaritan Flight to deliver the first planeload of relief items to Nicaragua. Janet personally distributed the lifesaving donations, traveling by four-wheel drive and mules into the hardest hit areas. Afterward she and Rosario Saavedra-Roman, a Nicaraguan-American whose father had been a pilot, used a $26,000 donation from the Greater Louisville Hurricane Relief Project to purchase $680,000 worth of medical supplies. Janet and Rosario personally distributed the supplies with the support of the Organization of American States.[29]

In January 2000 the Wings of Valor organization completed its 18th humanitarian mission to Nicaragua when an Air Force Reserve C-5 Galaxy landed in Managua full of donations of hospital equipment, clothes, school supplies, medicines, and other relief items. Volunteers from the Air Force Reserve's 482d Fighter Wing at Homestead AFB helped prepare the donations for shipment, and the Organization of American States' office in Nicaragua coordinated the distribution. Wings of Valor is a reflection of Janet Weininger's own deep sense of purpose and dedication to helping others. This is reflected in her words, "To be there for the forgotten is a mission of the heart."[30]

JANET RAY WEININGER's uplifting story reflects the special bond that exists among all of the veterans of the Bay of Pigs invasion and their families, whether they were born in the United States or whether they fled their homeland and eventually became naturalized U.S. citizens. Catherine Baker emphasized this special bond in 1982 when she told a reporter with *The Miami Herald* that she had applied for a visa to travel to Havana so she could lay flowers on the common grave where her husband Leo Baker's remains were buried. Enroute she planned to stop in Miami and place a bouquet at the monument for the fallen heroes in Little Havana. "They lost so much," she said of the Cuban exiles who fought at the Bay of Pigs. "I lost my husband. They lost a country."[31]

The Cuban exiles have enriched the culture and heritage of their new country. Demographically, their assimilation has spread far

Bay of Pigs veterans attending 117th Air Reconnaissance Wing banquet, May 13, 2000. (Left to Right) James C. Glenn, Louis H. Hudson, Charles R. Yates, Roy H. Wilson, Joseph L. Shannon, Joseph A. Fancher, Donald R. Crocker, William D. Bainbridge, Robert L. Stanley, William C. Fultz, Willie E. Colvert, John O. Spinks, William P. Baker, James W. Harrison, William R. Gray (AANG photo).

beyond Little Havana in Miami. A mid-1960s study of the first great exodus of perhaps 250,000 Cubans to the United States after Castro took power revealed that about half of these new immigrants settled in Florida, with all but 1,150 of those residing in the Miami area. Aided by the federal government and private groups, the other 125,000 Cubans spread to all of the other 49 states, with one refugee making it all the way to Alaska. The largest number, about 25,000, went to New York. About 235 settled in Alabama. This first wave of Cuban refugees and the thousands who followed have become a vibrant and integral part of our demographic makeup.[32]

Many of the younger Cuban males joined the U.S. Armed Forces when the Defense Department made special provisions for them to volunteer when President Kennedy ordered the military buildup during the Berlin Crisis. Prior to this, the exiles who wanted to join the armed forces were turned down because they were not U.S. citizens. The rush to join the armed forces continued after the Bay of Pigs veterans returned to the United States from Castro's prisons in December 1962. Some of them fought in Vietnam and made a career with the armed forces.[33]

Like warriors the world over, the men of Brigade 2506 look back on their baptism of fire at Cochinos Bay as a defining point in their lives. There are monuments and mementos to remind them lest they forget. There is a Useppa Island museum at Bokeelia, Florida, and a Bay of Pigs museum and library in Miami. When the Brigade's veterans hold a reunion, they religiously invite their comrades from the CIA and the Alabama Guard to join them. The monument in Little Havana for the fallen heroes is dedicated to the memory of the martyrs, including the four Alabama guardsmen, who gave their lives for Cuba's freedom.

Throughout forty years of honoring those martyrs, the brigade's veterans have never given up their dream of a free Cuba. Nor have they forgotten the pledge that President Kennedy made in January 1963 that someday the brigade's colors would fly over a free Cuba. They believe the president would have kept that promise—even though they still hold him responsible for the humiliating defeat at the Bay of Pigs—if he too had not been martyred on that sad day in Dallas in November 1963.

Back and front shots of Distinguished Intelligence Cross awarded posthumously to Riley Shamburger, Thomas Ray, Leo Baker, and Wade Gray (courtesy of Southern Museum of flight).

Appendix 1

Message Authorizing
Use of U.S. Aircrews at Bay of Pigs

Replica of sanitized message from HQ CIA to station chief at
Puerto Cabezas, Nicaragua:

> Washington, April 18, 1961, 11:26 a.m.
>
> 1. Following is for your guidance:
>
> A. Present air situation dictates following:
>
> (1) Maximum B-26 night attacks on strategic targets to elimi-
> nate Cuban air capability by Cuban crews.
>
> (2) Maximum resupply effort during hours of darkness Ameri-
> can to beachhead only and Cuban all area.
>
> (3) Use of F-51s in support of ground forces from Playa Giron.
>
> (4) Support of ground forces by American crews (over beach-
> head and sea approaches only).
>
> (5) Four additional B-26s being dispatched from Eglin to
> arrive evening 18 April.
>
> 2. American contract crews can be used B-26 strikes beach-
> head area and approaches only. Emphasize beachhead area only.
> Can not attach sufficient importance to fact American crews must
> not fall into enemy hands. In event this happens despite all
> precautions crews must state hired mercenaries, fighting commu-

nism, etc.; U.S. will deny any knowledge.

3. View above conserve all Cuban crews during daylight hours. Prepare for maximum effort strike tonight, Cuban crews frag bombs, three aircraft hit San Antonio de los Banos 19/0530Z and three additional aircraft strike same target 19/0700Z. Vary approaches effect maximum frag coverage all parking areas. Operational pattern future will be American air crews fly armed recce roads beachhead area approx each four hours. Cuban crews fly night airstrikes.

Note: Additional details on tonight's mission will follow.

Appendix 2

B-26 Aircrew Losses at the Bay of Pigs

April 15, 1961

Captain Daniel Fernandez-Mon and navigator Gaston Perez were killed during an attack on Libertad (Campo Columbia) base near Havana. Sustaining a direct hit from antiaircraft fire their B-26 exploded and crashed into the sea.

April 17, 1961

Captain Matias Farias was severely wounded and navigator Eddie Gonzalez killed when their B-26 was shot down by a T-33 piloted by Lieutenant Alberto Fernandez. Farias and Gonzalez were pursuing a Sea Fury fighter when Fernandez attacked them from behind.

Captain Raul Vianello went down with his B-26 after strafing Castro's field headquarters near the Australia sugar mill. The bomber was heavily damaged in an attack from a T-33 flown by Captain Alvaro Prendes. Navigator Demetrio Perez bailed out just before the damaged bomber crashed into the sea.

Captain Osvaldo Piedra and navigator Jose Fernandez died when their bomber was shot down by a T-33 in the vicinity of the

Australia sugar mill. The pilot of the T-33 was Lieutenant Alberto Fernandez.

Captain Jose Crespo and Lorenzo Perez-Lorenzo were killed when their badly damaged B-26 ditched in the sea before they could make it back to Puerto Cabezas. A Sea Fury flown by Lieutenant Douglas Rudd was credited with bringing the bomber down.

Captain Crispin Garcia and navigator Juan Gonzalez were returning to base when their bomber crashed into the coastal jungles of Nicaragua. After a Sea Fury attacked and damaged the B-26, Garcia made an emergency landing at Boca Chica in the Florida Keys to refuel before proceeding to Puerto Cabezas. Both men were killed in the crash. Later a third body, believed to be that of a stowaway, was discovered at the wreckage site.

April 19, 1961

Two Alabama guardsmen, Major Riley Shamburger and Wade Gray, were killed in action when a T-33 shot them down a few hundred yards offshore. Lieutenant Colonel Joseph Shannon saw the B-26 go into the water at high speed.

Captain Thomas W. Ray and Leo Baker were shot down while attacking inland targets near Castro's headquarters at the Australia sugar mill. Eyewitnesses stated that the two Alabama guardsmen survived the crash but were killed by Cuban militiamen.

Appendix 3

AANG Bay of Pigs Veterans

(‡ indicates deceased as of 2000.)

Members of the 117th*

William D. Baindridge

William P. Baker

Jack Bates

Robert Black‡

Warren E. Brown‡

John Burton

Donald F. Chandler‡

Willie E. Colvert

Donald R. Crocker

George R. Doster‡

Joseph A. Fancher

William C. Fultz

Thomas J. Gillespie‡

James C. Glenn

Billy J. Goodwin‡

William R. Gray

James W. Harrison

Ulay W. Littleton

Dalton Livingston‡

Theodore Marrs‡

Jack R. Mohon‡

Alvin Moore

William J. Pullen, Jr.‡

Freddie S. Raley

Thomas W. Ray‡

Riley Shamburger‡

Joseph L. Shannon

John O. Spinks

Robert L. Stanley

Benesdene L. Strawn‡

Carl N. Sudano

Carroll V. Sullivan‡

Charles Weldon

Bobby A. Whitley

Melvin Harvey‡   Roy H. Wilson

Louis H. Hudson   Charles R. Yates

Joel T. Kilgore‡

Members of the 187th**

Ernest Brantley‡   Hoyt Sproggins‡

Robert E. Harrison   Clarence Sullivan

David Hill‡   L. D. Thomas

Donald McIntyre‡   Willie B. Thompson‡

Jack Quinn   John R. Whetstone

Robert L. Scoggins

Others and Civilian Bay of Pigs Veterans***

List not available.

Notes:

*This roster of thirty-nine Bay of Pigs veterans who were members of the AANG 117th Air Refueling Wing (formerly the 117th Tactical Reconnaissance Wing) was compiled by the wing's public affairs office.

**Eleven AANG Bay of Pigs veterans were with the 187th Tactical Reconnaissance Group stationed at Dannelly Field in Montgomery, Alabama. The 117th Tactical Reconnaissance Wing was the parent unit of the 187th TRGp. The group was the antecedent of the 187th Fighter Wing, presently stationed at Dannelly Field. This list was provided by Bay of Pigs veterans Robert L. Scoggins and L. D. Thomas, who reside in Prattville, Alabama. According to Scoggins, who later served as senior enlisted advisor for the state of Alabama, the eleven Montgomery-area guardsmen were aircraft mechanics who were qualified on both single-engine and multi-engine aircraft. The 187th—having transitioned from RF-51 Mustangs and RF-80 Shooting Stars in the 1950s—was equipped with RF-84 jets. The eleven-man team from the 187th flew to Puerto Cabezas on March 29, 1961, with a larger group of guardsmen from the 117th Wing in Birmingham. They returned from Nicaragua on May 4, 1961, approximately two weeks after the Bay of Pigs invasion ended.

***Other volunteers recruited by the Air Guard commander for the covert CIA operation included some forty civilian pilots and technicians, primarily from the Birmingham area (a large number from Hayes Aircraft across the runway from the wing headquarters) for which there was no list available.

Notes

Introduction

[1] Edward B. Ferrer, *Operation Puma: The Air Battle of the Bay of Pigs* (Miami: Open Road Press, 1975), pp 213-14.

[2] Col Michael E. Haas, *Apollo's Warriors* (Maxwell AFB, AL: AU Press, 1997), pp 155, 157-59.

[3] Ibid., p 159; Ferrer, *Operation Puma*, pp 211-12; Joseph H. Shannon, interview by Don Dodd, Oct 7, 2000.

[4] Ferrer, *Operation Puma*, pp 213-14; Haynes Johnson, et al, *The Bay of Pigs: The Leaders' Story of Brigade 2506* (New York: W.W. Norton & Company, 1964), pp 154-55.

[5] Haas, *Apollo's Warriors*, p 159; Ferrer, *Operation Puma*, pp 215-16.

[6] Peter Wyden, *The Bay of Pigs: The Untold Story* (New York: Simon and Schuster, 1979), p 303.

[7] Ferrer, *Operation Puma*, p 213.

[8] Frank Sikora, "Alabama B-26 pilot recounts ill-fated Bay of Pigs invasion," *The Birmingham News*, May 6, 1998, p 1A.

[9] Mark Fineman and Dolly Mascarenas, "Bay of Pigs: The Secret Death of Pete Ray," *Los Angeles Times*, Sunday March 15, 1998, p 1.

[10] David L. Langford, "Alabama's role in Bay of Pigs invasion," *The Decatur Daily*, Sunday, April 13, 1986, p A-14.

Chapter 1

[1] Major General George Reid Doster Jr, biographical sketch, undated. General Doster's papers, 1943-1966, Auburn University Library; Wyden, *The Untold Story*, p 59.

[2] Tom Dolan, Alabama Historical Commission, "Brief Histories of the Governor's Mansions of Alabama," undated, pp 1, 3, 7, 10; Andrew Kilpatrick, "Patterson told secret Cuban invasion plans to JFK," *The Birmingham News*, undated, p 1A.

[3] Andrew Kilpatrick, "Patterson told secret Cuban invasion plans to candidate JFK," *The Birmingham News*, undated, p 1A.

[4] Earl Mazo, "Ike Speaks Out: Bay of Pigs was All JFK's," *Newsday*, Sep 10, 1965, p 50; Peter Gross, *Gentleman Spy: The Life of Allen Dulles* (Houghton Mifflin Company: Boston-New York, 1994), p 514.

[5] Kilpatrick, p 8A; Peter Kornbluh, ed., *Bay of Pigs Declassified: The Secret CIA Report on the Invasion of Cuba* (New York: The New Press, 1998), pp 273-74.

[6] "Debate Faubus Guard Charges," *Chicago's American*, March 7, 1963.

137

General Doster's papers, 1943-1966.

7 "Guard Pilots' Use Blasted," UPI press release, Little Rock, Ark., March 7, 1963. General Doster's papers, 1943-1966.

8 Ibid.

9 Lieutenant Colonel Joseph L. Shannon, interview by Warren Trest, Nov 3, 2000.

10 *The Southernaire*, Southern Airways, Feb 1944, pp 1,8; Chief Master Sergeant Roy H. Wilson, Ret., interview by Don Dodd, Oct 19, 2000; Milton "Buddy" Graves, interview by Don Dodd, Sep 22, 2000.

11 Kornbluh, *Bay of Pigs Declassified*, p 268; Grayston L. Lynch, *Decision for Disaster: Betrayal at the Bay of Pigs* (Washington & London: Brassey's, 1998), p 14.

12 Kornbluh, *Bay of Pigs Declassified*, p 258; Wyden, *Untold Story*, pp 69,70; Colonel Jack Hawkins, "An obsession with 'plausible deniability' doomed the 1961 Bay of Pigs invasion from the outset," *Military History*, Aug 1998, p 12.

13 Lynch, *Decision for Disaster*, p 21; Johnson, *The Leaders' Story*, pp 45, 46; Kornbluh, *Bay of Pigs Declassified*, p 273.

14 Haynes Johnson, et al, *The Bay of Pigs: The Leaders' Story of Brigade 2506* (New York: W.W. Norton & Company, Inc.: 1964), p 44; Lyman B. Kirkpatrick, Inspector General's Survey of the Cuban Operation, Oct 1961, p 126; Lieutenant Colonel Lowell S. Brennan, A Case Study of the Bay of Pigs, Air War College Report 4857, Apr 1973, p 12.

15 Kornbluh, *Bay of Pigs Declassified*, 273-75; Ronald Hilton, "The Retalhuleu Base," *The Hispanic American Report*, Vol 13, Nov 1960, p 583.

16 Kornbluh, *Bay of Pigs Declassified*, p 275.

17 Ibid., p 278; Ronald Hilton, "The Retalhuleu Base," *The Hispanic American Report*, Vol. 13, Nov 1960, p 583; Colonel Jack Hawkins, "An obsession with 'plausible deniability' doomed the 1961 Bay of Pigs invasion from the outset," *Military History*, Aug 1998, p 80; Joseph L. Shannon, interview by Don Dodd, Oct 5, 2000.

18 Haas, *Apollo's Warriors*, pp 153-54.

19 Ibid.; Warren A. Trest, *Air Commando One: Heinie Aderholt and America's Secret Air Wars* (Washington and London: Smithsonian Institution Press, 2000), p 113.

20 Haas, *Apollo's Warriors*, pp 153-54; William D. Bainbridge, interview by Don Dodd, Nov 25, 2000; Trest, *Air Commando One*, p 114.

21 Kornbluh, *Bay of Pigs Declassified*, pp 278-79.

22 Joseph L. Shannon, interview by Don Dodd, Oct 5, 2000; Albert C. Persons, *Bay of Pigs: A Firsthand Account of the Mission by a U.S. Pilot in Support of the Cuban Invasion Force in 1961* (Jefferson, North Carolina and London: McFarland & Company, Inc., 1990), p 62.

23 Haas, *Apollo's Warriors*, p 151; David L. Langford, AP Newsfeatures Writer, "Alabama's role in Bay of Pigs invasion," *The Decatur Daily*, Sunday, April 13, 1986, p A14.

[24] Sikora, "Alabama B-26 pilot," p 3A.

[25] Langford, *The Decatur Daily*, April 13, 1986; Dave Langford, "Fliers from city gambled lives, lost in Cuban attack," *The Birmingham News*, May 5, 1961; Dave Langford, "Four local airmen lost on flight for anti-Castro exiles," *The Birmingham News*, May 7, 1961; James W. "Jaws" Harrison, interview by Don Dodd, Sep 28, 2000.

[26] Wyden, *Untold Story*, p 61; Persons, *A Firsthand Account*, p 4; Albert C. Persons, "Inside Story on Cuba Invasion," *Chicago's American*, March 7, 1963, p 1.

[27] Persons, *Firsthand Account*, pp 5-7.

[28] John O. Spinks, interview by Don Dodd, Oct 20-21, 2000; Walter Bryant, "Guardsmen, buddies proudly marched into history," *The Birmingham News*, Nov 11, 2000, p 9A.

[29] Bobby A. Whitley, interview by Don Dodd, Oct 20, 2000.

[30] Chief Master Sergeant Roy H. Wilson, interview by Don Dodd, Oct 19, 2000.

[31] Ibid.

[32] Ibid.

[33] Langford, *The Decatur Daily*, April 13, 1986.

Chapter 2

[1] "The Big Build-up to Overthrow Castro," *U.S. News & World Report*," March 27, 1961, pp 44,45; Grose, *Gentleman Spy*, p 513.

[2] Johnson, et al, *The Leaders' Story*, 55-57; Ferrer, *Operation Puma*, 105-106; Lynch, *Decision for Disaster*, p 24; Wyden, *The Untold Story*, p 35.

[3] Lynch, *Decision for Disaster*, pp 24-25.

[4] Ibid.; Johnson, *The Leaders' Story*, p 61; Kornbluh, *Bay of Pigs Declassified*, p 286.

[5] Colonel William P. Baker, Air Guard (Ret.), interview by Don Dodd, Nov 6, 2000.

[6] Ibid; Louis H. Hudson, interview by Don Dodd, Nov 4, 2000; John O. Spinks interview by Don Dodd, Oct 20-21, 2000.

[7] Hudson interview, Nov 4, 2000.

[8] Baker interview, Nov 6, 2000.

[9] Hudson interview, Nov 4, 2000; James Glenn, interview by Don Dodd, Nov 7, 2000; Harrison interview, Sep 28, 2000; Bobby Whitley, interview by Don Dodd, Nov 11, 2000; Bill Gray, interview by Don Dodd, Nov 22, 2000.

[10] Hudson interview, Nov 4, 2000.

[11] Baker interview, Nov 6, 2000.

[12] Spinks interview, Oct 20-21, 2000; Glenn interview, Nov 7, 2000.

[13] Hudson interview, Nov 4, 2000.

[14] Persons, *Firsthand Account*, pp 15, 16, 23, 30.

[15] Ibid.; Wyden, *The Untold Story*, p 20, 62.

[16] Ferrer, *Operation Puma*, pp 17-30, 39, 52, 105.

[17] James Harrison, interview by Don Dodd, Oct 17, 2000; Hudson interview, Nov 4, 2000.

[18] Glenn interview, Nov 7, 2000; Whitley interview, Nov 11, 2000.

[19] David Wise and Thomas B. Ross, "The strange case of the CIA wid-

ows," *Look*, Jun 30, 1964, pp 77,78.

[20] James Glenn, interview by Don Dodd, Nov 7, 2000.

[21] Bainbridge interview, Nov 25, 2000.

[22] Ibid.

[23] Shannon interview, Nov 3, 2000; Whitley Interview, Oct 18, 2000; Bainbridge interview, Nov 25, 2000.

[24] Whitley interview, Oct 18, 2000.

[25] Ferrer, *Operation Puma*, pp 69, 70.

[26] Ibid, pp 105, 109; Captain Eduardo B. Ferrer, "If I Keep silent now, I'll regret it later!", *Diario Las Americas*, Sep 19, 1999, p 7-A.

[27] Ibid., p 109.

[28] Trest, *Air Commando One, pp 81, 82, 109-115.*

[29] Ferrer, *Operation Puma*, pp 109-10; Persons, *A Firsthand Account*, pp 53-54; Hudson interview, Nov 4, 2000; Whitley interview, Oct 18, 2000; Harrison interview, Oct 17, 2000.

[30] Ibid.; Haas, *Apollo's Warriors*, p 150; Dan Hagedorn and Leif Hellstrom, *Foreign Invaders: The Douglas Invader in Foreign Military and US Clandestine Service* (London: Midland Publishing Limited, 1994), pp 126-27.

[31] Glenn interview, Nov 7, 2000.

[32] Karl E. Meyer and Tad Szulc, *The Cuban Invasion: The Chronicle of a Disaster* (New York: Frederick A. Praeger, 1962), p 90.

[33] Theodore C. Sorensen, *Kennedy* (New York: Konecky & Konecky, 1965), p 295.

[34] Wyden, *The Untold Story*, pp 89,90; Lyman B. Kirkpatrick, Inspector General Survey of the Cuban Operation, 16 Feb 1962, p 22.

[35] Kirkpatrick, IG Survey, Annex B, p 7; Kornbluh, *Bay of Pigs Declassified*, pp 286-87.

[36] Kornbluh, pp 291-92.

[37] Ibid.

[38] Ibid., p 201; Meyer and Szulc, *The Cuban Invasion*, pp 96-105; Kirkpatrick, IG Survey, Annex B, pp 9-12.

[39] Richard M. Bissell, Jr., *Reflections of a Cold Warrior: From Yalta to the Bay of Pigs* (New Haven and London: Yale University Press, 1996), p 169.

[40] Colonel Jack Hawkins, "An obsession with 'plausible deniability' doomed the 1961 Bay of Pigs invasion from the outset," *Military History*, Aug 1998, p 81; Johnson, *The Leaders' Story*, p 67.

[41] Hawkins, *Military History*, p 80; Bissell, *Reflections*, p 170-71.

[42] Bissell, pp 170-71; Johnson, p 67; Evan Thomas, *The Very Best Men: The Early Years of the CIA* (New York: Simon & Schuster, 1995), p 251.

[43] Thomas, *Very Best Men*, p 251.

[44] Hawkins, p 80; Kornbluh, pp 265, 301.

[45] Ferrer, *Operation Puma*, pp 127, 143; Lynch, *Decision for Disaster*, pp 55-63.

[46] Lynch, pp 71-72; James G. Blight and Peter Kornbluh, *Politics of Illusion: The Bay of Pigs Reexamined* (Boulder, CO, and London: Lynne Rienner Publishers, 1998), p 94.

[47] Ferrer, pp 127, 143-45.

Chapter 3

1 Ferrer, *Operation Puma*, pp 138-39.

2 Bissell, *Reflections of a Cold Warrior*, p 183; Kornbluh, *Bay of Pigs Declassified*, p 303.

3 Ferrer, pp 138-39.

4 Shannon, interview by Dodd, Oct 5, 2000.

5 Message, Colonel Jack Hawkins to Richard Bissell, Apr 13, 1961, Annex A to Inspector General's Survey of the Cuban Operation, Oct 1961.

6 Ibid.

7 Shannon interview by Dodd, Oct 5, 2000.

8 Ferrer, pp 138-39.

9 Ibid, pp 140-41.

10 Ibid., pp 141-43, 147, 155; Kornbluh, p 303.

11 Shannon, interview by Dodd, Oct 7, 2000; Kornbluh, p 303; James G. Blight and Peter Kornbluh, *Politics of Illusion: The Bay of Pigs Invasion Reexamined* (Boulder, CO: Lynne Rienner Publishers, Inc., 1998), Appendix 5: Declassified Documents, pp 235-36.

12 Ferrer, pp 151-58.

13 Ibid., "Cuba: The Massacre," *Time*, Apr 28, 1961, pp 19,20.

14 Ferrer, pp 158-60; Kornbluh, pp 303, 304.

15 Blight and Kornbluh, *Politics of Illusion*, p 236; Kornbluh, p 303; Wyden, p 170.

16 Bobby A. Whitley, interview by Don Dodd, Oct 18, 2000.

17 Blight and Kornbluh, p 237; Kornbluh, p 305; Colonel Jack Hawkins, "An obsession with 'plausible deniability' doomed the 1961 Bay of Pigs invasion from the outset," *Military History*, Aug 1998, p 80.

18 Ferrer, p 162; Joseph Shannon interview, Nov 3, 2000.

19 Bissell, *Reflections of a Cold Warrior*, p 185.

20 Ibid., p 184.

21 Grayston L. Lynch, *Decision for Disaster* (Washington and London: Brassey's, 1998), pp 67, 83-85.

22 Ibid., pp 65, 70, 71; John Barry, "CIA's man at the Bay of Pigs," *Miami Herald*, Jul 16, 1998.

23 Lynch, *Decision for Disaster*, p 87; Haynes Johnson, *The Bay of Pigs: The Leaders' Story of Brigade 2506* (New York: W.W. Norton & Company, Inc., 1964), p 105.

24 Johnson, p 110; Kornbluh, p 304.

25 Ferrer, pp 169-70.

26 Roy Wilson interview, Oct 19, 2000.

27 Johnson, pp 111-12.

28 Ibid., p 113; Kornbluh, pp 310-11; Lynch, pp 111-17; Ferrer, pp 202-203.

29 Kornbluh, p 310.

30 Lynch, p 113.

31 Ferrer, pp 190-91, 196-97.

32 Kornbluh, p 311.

33 Ferrer, pp 203-204; Dan Hagedorn and Leif Hellstrom, *Foreign Invaders: The Douglas Invader in foreign military and US clandestine service* (Oxford, England: The Alden Press, 1994), p 130.

34 Hudson interview, Nov 4, 2000; Don Crocker, interview by Don Dodd,

Jan. 13, 2001.

[35] Ferrer, *Operation Puma*, pp 187-90

Chapter 4.

[1] Telegram, Central Intelligence Agency to personnel in Nicaragua, Washington, Apr 18, 1961, loc CIA, DCI Files: Job 85-00664R, Box 4, Vol. I.

[2] Memo, McGeorge Bundy, special asst for national security affairs, to President John F. Kennedy, Washington, Apr 18, 1961, loc Kennedy Library, President's Office Files, Countries Series, Cuba, General, Apr 1961.

[3] Ibid.; Karl E. Meyer and Tad Szulc, *The Cuban Invasion: The Chronicle of a Disaster* (New York: Frederick A. Praeger, 1962), p. 136.

[4] Meyer and Szulc, *The Cuban Invasion*, p 137.

[5] Message, CIA to Nicaragua, Apr 18, 1961.

[6] Ibid.

[7] Ferrer, *Operation Puma*, pp 205-06; Johnson, *The Leaders' Story*, p 140.

[8] Lynch, *Decision for Disaster*, p 121.

[9] Ibid., p 123.

[10] Ibid., pp 124-25.

[11] Ferrer, *Operation Puma*, p 207; Haas, *Apollo's Warriors*, p 159.

[12] Ferrer, p 207; Haas, p 159.

[13] Ferrer, *Operation Puma*, p 208.

[14] Ibid.

[15] Persons, *A Firsthand Account*, pp 89-90.

[16] Ibid., p 90; Ferrer, p 213; David L. Langford, Associated Press, "Pilot recalls futility of air battle," *Las Ve-gas Review-Journal*, Sunday, Apr 13, 1986, p 19A.

[17] Langford, *Las Vegas Review-Journal*, p 19A.

[18] Arthur M. Schlesinger, Jr., *A Thousand Days—John F. Kennedy in the White House* (Boston: Houghton-Mifflin Company, 1965); Captain William C. Chapman, USN ret., Author's Comments, "The Bay of Pigs: The View from Prifly," A paper to be presented at the Ninth Naval History Symposium, U.S. Naval Academy, Oct 20, 1989; Peter Wyden, *Bay of Pigs: The Untold Story* (New York: Simon and Schuster, 1979), p 299.

[19] Ferrer, *Operation Puma*, pp 214-16; Langford, *Las Vegas Review-Journal*, p 19A.

[20] Bill Gray interview, Nov 22, 2000.

[21] Ferrer, pp 214-15; Langford, p 19A; Statement by Joe Shannon, Dec 8, 2000.

[22] Willie Colvert, interview by Don Dodd, Nov 29, 2000.

[23] Carl Sudano, interview by Don Dodd, Dec 9, 2000.

[24] Persons, *A Firsthand Account*, p 95.

[25] Ibid., p 97.

[26] Ibid., 97-100; Langford, *Las Vegas Review-Journal, Apr 13, 1986, p 19A.*

[27] Persons, p 112; Langford, p 19A; Bobby A. Whitley, interview by Don Dodd, Oct 18, 2000; Roy H. Wilson, interview by Don Dodd, Oct 19, 2000.

[28] Johnson, *The Leaders' Story*, p 143; Lynch, *Decision for Disaster*, p 131; Major Donald L. Moore, USMCR, "The Bay of Pigs: An Analysis,"

Naval War College Review, Nov 1966, p 24.

29 "The Price of Military Folly," *U.S. News & World Report*, Apr 22, 1996, pp 53-56.

30 "The Real Story of the Bay of Pigs," *U.S. News & World Report*, Jan 7, 1963, pp 38-41; Professor Lyman B. Kirkpatrick, Jr., "Paramilitary Case Study: The Bay of Pigs," *Naval War College Review*, Nov-Dec 1972, p 38.

31 Ferrer, *Operation Puma*, pp 219-21.

32 James Glenn, interview by Don Dodd, Nov 7, 2000; Interviews with Don Crocker, Bill Fultz, Fred Raley, Bob Stanley, and Charles Yates, Jan 12-13, 2001.

33 Bobby Whitley interview, Oct 18, 2000.

Chapter 5

1 James W. Harrison, interview by Don Dodd, Oct 17, 2000.

2 Persons, *Firsthand Account*, p 114.

3 Frank Sikora, "Alabama B-26 pilot recounts ill-fated Bay of Pigs invasion," *The Birmingham News*, May 6, 1998, p 1A.

4 David L. Langford, "Bay of Pigs: Waterloo of the CIA," *Las Vegas Review-Journal*, Sunday, Apr 13, 1986, p 20A.

5 Ibid; Dave Langford, "Fliers from city gambled lives, lost in Cuban attack," *The Birmingham News*, May 5, 1961; Dave Langford, "Four local airmen lost on flight for anti-Castro exiles," *Birmingham News*, May 7, 1961, p 1.

6 Langford, *Birmingham News*, May 5, 1961; David Wise and Thomas B. Ross, "The Strange Case of the CIA Widows," *Look*, Jun 30, 1964, pp 78,79.

7 Wise and Ross, *Look*, Jun 30, 1964, p 78; Lillian Foscue, "4 Pilots 'CIA Airmen,' Magazine Reports," *Birmingham Post-Herald*, Jun 16, 1964.

8 Wise and Ross, *Look*, Jun 30, 1964, p 80.

9 Foscue, *Birmingham Post-Herald*, Jun 16, 1964.

10 "How Remark Led American to the Story," *Chicago's American*, Mar 7, 1963, p 1.

11 Ibid; Department of Air Force Special Order, S.O. AA1761, Jul 31, 1964.

12 Wise and Ross, *Look*, Jun 30, 1964, pp 83,84.

13 Albert C. Persons, "Inside Story of Cuba Invasion," *Chicago's American*, Mar 7, 1963, p 1.

14 Ibid.

15 Wise and Ross, *Look*, p 84; Foscue, *Birmingham Post-Herald*, p 1.

16 "The Price of Military Folly," *U.S. News & World Report*, Apr 22, 1996, p 56.

17 "Won't desert Cuba to Reds, warns JFK," *The Birmingham News*," Apr 20, 1961, p 1.

18 Ibid.

19 Bissell, *Reflections of a Cold Warrior*, p 193.

20 Captain Eduardo B. Ferrer, "If I Keep silent now, I'll regret it later!", *Diario Las Americas*, Sep 19, 1999, p 7-A.

21 Ibid.

22 "Bay of Pigs Revisited," *Time*, Feb 1, 1963, p 11.

23 Arthur M. Schlesinger Jr., "The Bay of Pigs—'A Horribly Expensive Lesson'," *Life*, Jul 23, 1965, p 64.

24 Ferrer, *Operation Puma*, p 137.

25 Bissell, *Reflections of a Cold Warrior*, p 194.

26 Colonel Jack Hawkins, "An obsession with 'plausible deniability' doomed the 1961 Bay of Pigs invasion from the outset," *Military History*, Aug 1998, p 80.

27 Ibid.

28 "Cuba: The Massacre," *Time*, Apr 28, 1961, p 19.

29 Keith Wheeler, "'Hell of a Beating' in Cuba," *Life*, Apr 28, 1961, pp 17-19.

30 Ibid.

31 Maurice Halperin, *The rise and Decline of Fidel Castro* (Berkely: University of California Press, 1972), pp 109, 111-12.

32 Haynes Johnson, *The Bay of Pigs: The Leaders' Story of Brigade 2506* (New York: W. W. Norton and Co., 1964), pp 229-37.

33 Ibid., pp 231-33.

34 Howard Handleman, "Prisoners Tell—The Real Story of the Bay of Pigs," *U.S. News & World Report*, Jan 7, 1963, pp 38-41.

35 "Cubans Try Dothanite, Five Others," *Montgomery Advertiser*, Jan 29, 1961; "Dothan man stirs hopes for release," *Birmingham News*, Feb 1, 1961.

36 "Dothan man, five companions on trial in Cuba," *Birmingham News*, Jan 28, 1961, p 1; "Alabama man jailed in Cuba, writes goodby," *Birmingham News*, Jan 20, 1961, p 1.

37 *Birmingham News*, Feb 1, 1964.

38 Max McGowan, "Cuba Swap Negotiator Hopes To Get Dothan Man Released," *The Montgomery Advertiser*, Mar 31, 1963; "Plane like angel to Alabamian; ex-prisoners tell of eating cats," *The Birmingham News*, Apr 23, 1963, p 4.

39 James Marlow, "What's Sauce for U.S. Becomes So for Reds," *The Birmingham News*, Apr 23, 1963, p 4; Max McGowan, "Tired, Happy Tommy Baker Meets Family," *The Montgomery Advertiser*, Apr 23, 1963.

40 Cecil B. Currey, *The Unquiet American* (Washington/London: Brassey's, 1998), pp 239-51.

Chapter 6.

1 James Harrison, interview by Don Dodd, Oct 17, 2000.

2 Charles Joseph Gross, *Prelude to the Total Force: The Air National Guard 1943-1969* (Washington, D.C.: Office of Air Force History, 1985), p 126; Robert Frank Futrell, *Ideas, Concepts, Doctrine: Basic Thinking in the United States Air Force 1961-1984, Vol II* (Maxwell AFB, AL: Air University Press, 1989), p 36.

3 Ibid., p 128; David L. Langford, "Alabama's role in Bay of Pigs invasion," *The Decatur Daily*, Sunday Morning, Apr 13, 1986, p A14; Department of Air Force Special Order AA1761, Jul 31, 1964; Alabama Special Order 116, Jun 21, 1966.

[4] James Bennett, "Air Guard Hauling of Whiskey Probed," *Birmingham Post-Herald*, Jan 16, 1965, p 1; James Bennett, "Wallace Issues Order on Liquor," *Birmingham Post-Herald*, Jan 22, 1965, p 1.

[5] James Bennett, "Gen. Doster Named in $100,000 Suit," *Birmingham Post-Herald*, Mar 30, 1965, p 1.

[6] "Doster Trial Opens Here On Monday," *The Montgomery Advertiser*, Aug 20, 1972, p 1.

[7] Ibid; "Doster File Growing as Both Sides Angle for Position," *The Montgomery Advertiser*, Jul 6, 1972, p 17; M. P. Weisskopf, "Motion to Move Doster Trial Denied," *The Montgomery Advertiser*, Jul 7, 1972, p 2; "Judge Denies Venue Change For Doster," *The Montgomery Advertiser*, Jul 19, 1972, p 16; "Doster, Four Others Go On Federal Trial Today," *The Montgomery Advertiser*, Aug 21, 1972, p 1.

[8] M. P. Weisskopf, "U.S. to Drop Cases After Doster Quits," *The Montgomery Advertiser*, Aug 22, 1972, p 1,2.

[9] Judge Ira DeMent, interview by Don Dodd, Dec 7, 2000.

[10] Ibid.; David L. Langford, "Alabama's Role in Bay of Pigs Invasion," p 1; Harrison interview, Oct 17, 2000.

[11] Kathleen Henderson, "Aviation tour guide won't take flying for granted," *The Birmingham News*, Feb 28, 1996, p 11S.

[12] Sudano interview, Dec 9, 2000.

[13] Walter Bryant, "CIA honors servicemen in Bay of Pigs Invasion," *The Birmingham News*, Jan. 21, 2001, p 19A.

[14] Letter, Colonel Kirk J. Tyree, AL ANG, Commander, 117th Air Refueling Wing, to Mr. Joseph L. Shannon, Sep 19, 2000.

[15] John Arnold, "Young Bay of Pigs Pilot Returns to a Long-Delayed Funeral," *The Miami Herald*, Dec 6, 1979, p 1.

[16] Ibid; "Bay of Pigs Pilot's Body Is Identified," *The Miami Herald*, Sep 5, 1979, p 10-F.

[17] Arnold, *The Miami Herald*, Dec 6, 1979, p 1.

[18] Ibid.

[19] Mark Fineman and Dolly Mascarenas, "Bay of Pigs: The Secret Death of Pete Ray," *Los Angeles Times*, Mar 14, 1998.

[20] Ted Gup, *The Washington Post*, Jul 9, 1999, p WO6; Ted Gup, *The Book of Honor* (New York: Doubleday, 2000), pp 117-25.

[21] Jaffe/Point Productions, *Top Secret Missions of the CIA, 102: Puma*, undated; Fineman and Mascarenas, *Los Angeles Times*, Mar 14, 1998; Jay M. Glass, Chief Deputy Coroner, Birmingham, AL, interview by Don Dodd, Jun 27, 1999.

[22] Liz Balmaseda, "Her long vigil ends in a common grave," *The Miami Herald*, May 15, 1982, p 1,6.

[23] Vanessa Rauza, " "39 years after Bay of Pigs, bodies of two pilots to be returned to Miami for burial," *Sun-Sentinel*, Oct 18, 2000.

[24] Evan Thomas, "On the Trail of Truth," *Newsweek*, May 11, 1998, p 37.

[25] Ibid; Shannon interview, Oct 5, 2000; Glenn Garvin, "One last flight for

two pilots," *The Miami Herald*, Mar 16, 1998.

[26] Evan Thomas, "*Newsweek*, May 11, 1998, p 37; Sue Mullin, "Crusading housewife strives for Bay of Pigs closure, *The Washington Times*, Apr 12, 1998, pp 2,6.

[27] Vanessa Rauza, *Sun-Sentinel*, Oct 18, 2000.

[28] Circular on Wings of Valor, undated; Letter To Whom It May Concern, from Lucia Cardenal de Salazar, Consul General of Nicaragua, undated.

[29] Circular on Wings of Valor, undated; Letter, U.S. Ambassador Lino Gutierrez to Mr. Dennis Dolan, Greater Louisville Hurricane Relief Project, Dec 11, 1998; Glenn Garvin, "From Miami with love, planeload of aid arrives," *The Miami Herald*, Nov 17, 1998.

[30] Circular on Wings of Valor, undated; Letter, U.S. Congresswoman Ileana Ros-Lehtinen to Ms Janet Ray Weininger, Apr 19, 2000.

[31] Liz Balmaseda, "Her long vigil ends in a common grave," *The Miami Herald,* May 15, 1982, pp 1,6.

[32] Richard F. Newcomb, "Where Cuban Refugees Are," *The Atlanta Journal,* Oct 31, 1965.

[33] "Cuban Youths Flock To Join U.S. Army For Any Action," *Birmingham Post-Herald,* Oct 24, 1962; "U.S. Military Will Now Accept Cuban Refugees," *Montgomery Advertiser,* Jul 29, 1961.

Bibliography

Authors' Bibliographic Notes

Historians relish sinking their teeth into the meat of a failed military campaign, especially one that is a consequence of strategic blunders from on high. Couple this generality with the Fourth Estate's disdain for the CIA's culture of secrecy, and we have in the Bay of Pigs debacle—defined as a "perfect failure" by one author—a uniquely American military tragedy and an intellectual bonanza for scholars. This is reflected in the outpouring of books and articles on the failed Bay of Pigs invasion, as well as the sharing of critical information and documentation over the internet. These secondary sources and a series of interviews with participants have been indispensable to writing this volume about the Alabama Air National Guard's covert role in the ill-fated invasion.

Learning the hard lessons from our failures on the battlefield is what military history is all about. Two books that explore the lessons learned from the liberation air force's operations in support of the Cuban invasion are (1) *Operation Puma: The Air Battle of the Bay of Pigs*, by Edward B. Ferrer, and (2) *Bay of Pigs: A Firsthand Account of the Mission by a U.S. Pilot in Support of the Cuban Invasion Force in 1961*, by Albert C. "Buck" Persons. Edward Ferrer, a member of the special group of Cuban exiles who flew in support of the invasion, has written a fascinating memoir of the total air experience at the Bay of Pigs. *Operation Puma*, self-published with a foreword by Admiral Arleigh Burke, is in its fourth printing in Spanish and its second printing in English. The author writes with compassion and lets the chips fall where they may. His insightful book is a valuable source of information for students of air power in limited war situations, particularly those having an interest in the air battle at the Bay of Pigs.

Person's memoir, also self-published, centers on the experiences of the Alabama advisers who were involved with the invasion. The author, now deceased, was a veteran military pilot and journalist who became the managing editor of a weekly newspaper, the *Birmingham Examiner*, after returning from the secret CIA mission in support of the invasion. Like Ferrer's book, Person's narrative pulls no punches but his use of pseudonyms, as required by CIA rules governing the Bay of Pigs operation, rather than the real names of the American advisers makes the narrative difficult to follow. What Person's book lacks in clarity it makes up for in depth of coverage about the role of Alabama volunteers in the invasion. It is another essential source of information for anyone who is researching or writing about air operations at the Bay of Pigs.

A third memoir, *Decision for Disaster: Betrayal at the Bay of Pigs* by Grayston L. Lynch, is one of the best books yet to appear on the subject. Despite White House orders that no Americans were to go into harm's way at the Bay of Pigs, Lynch led a small group of frogmen ashore at the outset of the invasion and fired the first shots against the Cuban militia. For the next three days he was aboard the command ship *Blagar* where he was an eyewitness to the entire three-day battle between the Cuban exile brigade and Castro's forces. *Decision for Disaster* is a fascinating, action-packed account of the battle that must be read by anyone who wants to understand what the brigade went through at the Bay of Pigs and the lessons to be learned from that experience.

An equally important book about the Cuban brigade is Haynes

Johnson's *The Bay of Pigs: The Leaders' Story of Brigade 2506*. The author did his homework before writing the brigade's story with the help of four prominent brigade leaders—Manuel Artime, political leader; Jose Perez San Roman, the brigade commander; Erneido Oliva, and Enrique Ruiz-Williams. The book is a goldmine of firsthand information about the Bay of Pigs, much of which is not readily attainable from other sources. The book helps us to fully understand what these courageous men went through in the hopes of freeing their homeland.

Perhaps the best known and most readable of the books about the Cuban invasion is Peter Wyden's *Bay of Pigs: The Untold Story*. Wyden's skillfully crafted narrative entertains and informs us. It brings the Bay of Pigs story alive with vivid action and colorful portraits of both protagonists and antagonists—giving us more than a one-dimensional view of a defining moment in John F. Kennedy's presidency and U.S.-Cuba relations. Wyden developed his hard-hitting narrative through access to a wide range of key individuals involved in the Bay of Pigs failure—from the decisionmaking halls of Washington, D.C. and Havana to the lowliest grunts on the battlefield. Even those who are not engaged in a serious study of the Bay of Pigs might want to read Wyden's book just for the pleasure of it.

A scholarly work that stands out for its clarity, synthesis, and historical analysis is *The Cuban Invasion: The Chronicle of a Disaster* by Karl E. Meyer and Tad Szulc. Compressed into this 156-page volume is a comprehensive view that one might not obtain by studying a wide variety of other sources. Scholars who are thinking of researching and writing about the Bay of Pigs will benefit from reading Meyer's and Szulc's work first. The same might be said for Chapter Seven (pages 152-204) of Richard M. Bissell, Jr.'s memoirs *Reflections of a Cold Warrior: From Yalta to the Bay of Pigs*. Bissell's reflections on the Bay of Pigs should be read with a discerning eye, however, because they are in part an apologia giving his side of the story about events leading to "the perfect failure."

Peter Grose's biography of Allen Dulles, *Gentleman Spy* adds little to our understanding of the CIA director's detached attitude toward "the perfect failure" that ended his career. If nothing else, the biography clearly shows that the Bay of Pigs was but a blip on the radar screen of Dulles's national security concerns and his decades of distinguished service to his country. The same could be said of Theodore C. Sorensen's *Kennedy*; James L. Binder's *Lemnitzer: A Soldier for his Time*; Maxwell D. Taylor's *Swords and Plowshares*; and Cecil B. Currey's *Edward Lansdale: The Unquiet American*. Each of these works contains one or two illuminating nuggets about "the perfect failure," but novice researchers run the risk of striking fool's gold.

Two less important works that looked promising but fizzled out were *Give Us This Day* by Howard Hunt and *Counter-Revolutionary Agent: Diary of the events which occurred in Cuba between January and July 1961* by Hans Tanner. Making up for these disappointments were two recent books that proved indispensable: *Bay of Pigs Declassified: The Secret CIA Report on the Invasion of Cuba* edited by Peter Kornbluh, and *Politics of Illusion: The Bay of Pigs Invasion Reexamined* edited by James G. Blight and Peter Kornbluh. These volumes contain insightful analyses gleaned from interviews with key government officials involved with the Bay of Pigs at the command level. They should be studied in conjunction with the *Inspector General's Survey of the Cuban Operation and Associated Documents* released as sanitized in 1997 by the CIA and reprinted by The National Security Archive at George Washington University, Washington, D.C.

Two other works that provide useful information on the air battle at the Bay of Pigs are *Apollo's Warriors: United States Air Force Special Operations during the Cold War* by Colonel Michael E. Haas, USAF Retired, and *Foreign Invaders: The Douglas Invader in foreign military and US clandestine service* by Dan Hagedorn and Leif Hellstrom. Both books have chapters devoted to the B-26 strikes that were planned and executed by the CIA against Castro's forces during the Cuban invasion.

A variety of magazine and newspaper articles were consulted in writing this book. *Time, Newsweek, U.S. News and World Report, Look, and Life* were among the principal magazine sources cited in the narrative. The authors drew extensively from two major Alabama newspapers: *The Birmingham News* and *The Montgomery Advertiser.* Particularly helpful were insightful features written by ace Birmingham reporters David L. Langford, Associated Press newsfeature writer, and Frank Sikora, *Birmingham News* staff writer. Other useful sources were *The Birmingham Post-Herald*, *Chicago's American*, *The Decatur Daily*, *The Examiner*, *Las Vegas Review-Journal*, and *The Miami Herald*.

Official government agencies consulted were the Air National Guard History office in Washington, D.C.; the State of Alabama Archives & History, Montgomery, Alabama; and the Air Force Historical Research Agency and the Air University Library at Maxwell AFB, Alabama. On file at the Air University Library are a number of excellent theses on the Bay of Pigs prepared by officers attending the Air War College and the Air Command and Staff College. The personal papers collection of Major General George Reid Doster, located in the Auburn University Library, contains little information about the general's role in the Bay of Pigs—only a few articles that were clipped from magazines and newspapers. Most useful were a series of interviews with Alabama Air National Guard veterans of the Bay of Pigs in October and November 2000 by Don Dodd, with the Southern Museum of Flight in Birmingham, Alabama.

Books

Binder, L. James. *Lemnitzer: A Soldier for his Time.* Washington and London: Brassey's, 1997.

Bissell, Richard M. Jr. *Reflections of a Cold Warrior: From Yalta to the Bay of Pigs.* New Haven and London: Yale University Press, 1996.

Blight, James G. and Peter Kornbluh. *The Bay of Pigs Invasion Reexamined.* Boulder and London: Lynne Rienner Publishers, 1998.

Corn, David. *Blond Ghost: Ted Shackley and the CIA's Crusades.* New York: Simon & Schuster, 1994.

Currey, Cecil B. *Edward Lansdale: The Unquiet American.* Washington and London: Brassey's, 1998.

Dodd, Don and Amy Bartlett-Dodd. *Deep South Aviation.* Charleston, SC: Arcadia Publishing, 1999.

Ferrer, Edward B. *Operation Puma: The Air Battle at the Bay of Pigs.* Miami: Open Road Press, 1975.

Grose, Peter. *Gentleman Spy: The Life of Allen Dulles.* Boston and New York: Houghton Mifflin Company, 1994.

Gup, Ted. *The Book of Honor: Covert Lives and Classified Deaths at the CIA.* New York: Doubleday, 2000.

Haas, Michael E. *Apollo's Warriors: United States Air Force Special Operations during the Cold War.* Maxwell AFB, AL: Air University Press, 1997.

Hagedorn, Dan and Leif Hellstrom. *Foreign Invaders: The Douglas Invader in foreign military and US clandestine operations.* London: Midland Publishing Ltd., 1994.

Halperin, Maurice. *The Rise and Decline of Fidel Castro.* Berkeley: University of California Press, 1972.

Hunt, Howard. *Give Us This Day.* New Rochelle, N.Y.: Arlington House, 1973.

Johnson, Haynes, et al. *The Bay of Pigs: The Leaders' Story of Brigade 2506.* New York: Random House, 1991.

Kornbluh, Peter, ed. *Bay of Pigs Declassified: The Secret CIA Report on the Invasion of Cuba.* New York: The New Press, 1998.

Lynch, Grayston L. *Decision for Disaster: Betrayal at the Bay of Pigs.* Washington and London: Brassey's, 1998.

Meyer, Karl E. and Tad Szulc. *The Cuban Invasion: The Chronicle of a Disaster.* New York: Frederic A. Praeger, 1962.

Persons, Albert C. *Bay of Pigs: A Firsthand Account of the Mission by a U.S. Pilot in Support of the Cuban Invasion Force in 1961.* Jefferson N.C.: McFarland & Company, Inc., 1990.

Ranelagh, John. *CIA: A History.* London: BBC Books, 1992.

Salisbury, Harrison E. *Without Fear or Favor.* New York: The New York Times Book Co., Inc., 1980.

Sorensen, Theodore C. *Kennedy.* New York: Konecky & Konecky, 1965.

Tanner, Hans. *Counter-Revolutionary Agent: Diary of the events which occurred in Cuba between January and July 1961.* London: G.T. Foulis & Co., Ltd, 1962.

Taylor, Gen. Maxwell D. *Swords and Plowshares.* New York: Da Capo

Press, Inc., 1972.

Thomas, Evan. *The Very Best Men. Four Who Dared: The Early Years of the CIA.* New York: Simon & Schuster, 1995.

Wyden, Peter. *The Bay of Pigs: The Untold Story.* New York: Simon & Schuster, 1979.

Articles

"Alabama man jailed in Cuba, writes goodby." *The Birmingham News* (January 20, 1961).

"Alabama Pilots Shot Down in Cuba Praised in Letter." *The Montgomery Advertiser* (August 3, 1963).

Barry, John. "CIA's man at the Bay of Pigs." *The Miami Herald* (July 16, 1998).

"Bay of Pigs Disaster." *Reporter* (February 14, 1963).

"Bay of Pigs Revisited." *Time* (February 1, 1963).

Benedetto, Richard. "An Invasion of Bad Ideas." *USA Today* (June 23, 1997).

"Bitter Week: Cuban Invasion." *Time* (April 28, 1961).

"Castro Holding Dothanite's Fate." *The Montgomery Advertiser* (January 20, 1961).

Chapman, Capt. William C. "The Bay of Pigs: The View from Prifly." *U.S. Naval Institute Proceedings* (October 1992).

"CIA portrayed as credit, embarrassment to nation." *The Montgomery Advertiser* (September 14, 1997).

"Cuban Situation Spawns Storm of Talk in Miami." *The Montgomery Adver-*

tiser (April 24, 1961).

"Cubans Try Dothanite, Five Others." *The Montgomery Advertiser* (January 29, 1961)

"D-Day in Cuba." *The Montgomery Advertiser* (April 18, 1961).

Dominguez, Eddie. "Bay of Pigs vets take stroll in time." *The Birmingham News* (April 21, 1997).

"Doster File Growing as Both Sides Angle for Position." *The Montgomery Advertiser* (July 6, 1972).

"Doster, Four Others Go On Federal Trial Today." *The Montgomery Advertiser* (August 21, 1972).

"Doster Trial Opens Here On Monday." *The Montgomery Advertiser* (August 20, 1972).

"Dothan man, five companions on trial in Cuba." *The Birmingham News* (January 28, 1961).

"Dothan man jailed in Cuba, fears future means Castro firing squad." *The Birmingham News* (January 19, 1961).

"Dothan man stirs hopes for release." *The Birmingham News* (February 1, 1961).

"Excerpts From Bay of Pigs Report." *New York Times* (February 22, 1998).

"Fiasco in Cuba." *The Nation* (June 24, 1961).

Fineman, Mark and Dolly Mascarenas. "Bay of Pigs: The Secret Death of Pete Ray." *Los Angeles Times* (March 14, 1998).

Foscue, Lillian. "4 Pilots 'CIA Airmen,' Magazine Reports." *The Birmingham Post Herald* (June 16, 1964).

"General Doster Identified as Invasion

Air Chief." *The Birmingham Post-Herald* (March 8, 1963).

"Ghosts and Reality: U.S. Air Cover for Bay of Pigs Beachhead." *Newsweek* (February 4, 1963).

Hawkins, Col. Jack, USMC. "An obsession with 'plausible deniability' doomed the 1961 Bay of Pigs invasion from the outset." *Military History* (August 1998).

Higgins, Marguerite. "On the Spot: In Defense of the CIA." *Newsday* (September 10, 1965).

"How President Kennedy Upset Cuban Invasion of April 1961." *U.S. News & World Report* (February 4, 1963).

"Judge Denies Venue Change For Doster." *The Montgomery Advertiser* (July 19, 1972).

Kilpatrick, Andrew. "Patterson told secret Cuban invasion plans to candidate JFK." *The Birmingham News*, undated.

Kirkpatrick, Lyman B. Jr. "Paramilitary Case Study: The Bay of Pigs." *Naval War College Review* (November-December 1972).

Langford, Dave. "Fliers from city gambled lives, lost in Cuban attack." *The Birmingham News* (May 5, 1961).

_____. "Four local airmen lost on flight for anti-Castro exiles." *The Birmingham News* (May 7, 1961).

Langford, David L. "Alabama's role in Bay of Pigs invasion." *The Decatur Daily* (April 13, 1986).

_____. "Pilot recalls futility of air battle." *Las Vegas Review-Journal* (April 13, 1986)

Marlow, James. "What's Sauce for U.S. Becomes So For Reds." *The Birmingham News* (April 23, 1963).

McGowan, Max. "Cuba Swap Negotiator Hopes To Get Dothan Man Released." *The Montgomery Advertiser* (March 31, 1963).

_____. "Tired, Happy Tommy Baker Meets Family." *The Montgomery Advertiser* (April 23, 1963).

"Mom Thrilled At Word Son To Return." *The Birmingham Post-Herald* (April 22, 1963)

Moore, Maj. Donald L, USMC. "The Bay of Pigs: An Analysis." *Naval War College Review* (November 1966).

Muckerman, Col. Joseph E. II, USA. "Bay of Pigs Revisited." *Military Review* (April 1971).

Nelson, Craig. "CIA report takes blame for Bay of Pigs." *USA Today* (February 23, 1998).

Persons, Albert C. "Inside Story of Cuba Invasion." *Chicago's American* (March 7, 1963).

_____. "Report 2 Days of Indecision, Then U.S. Halted Cuba Air Cover." *Chicago's American* (March 8, 1963).

_____. "The Bay of Pigs: Revived, Remade, Resold (Part One of a Two-part Article)." *The Examiner* (September 24, 1964).

_____. "The Bay of Pigs: Revived, Remade, Resold (Part Two of a Two-part Article)." *The Examiner* (September 25, 1964).

_____. "U.S. Fliers Died at Bay of Pigs." *The Examiner* (February 3, 1963).

"Plane like angel to Alabamians; ex-prisoners tell of eating cats." *The Birmingham News* (April 23, 1963).

"Prisoners tell the Real Story of the Bay of Pigs." *U.S. News & World Report* (January 7, 1963).

"Prisoner's Mother Seeks JFK's Help." *The Birmingham Post-Herald* (January 30, 1961).

Reich, Peter. "Jet Could Have Saved the Day, Says General." *Chicago's American* (March 8, 1963).

Ryan, William L. "April Disaster May Be Repeat of Cuban History." *The Montgomery Advertiser* (April 21, 1961).

Sewell, Dan. "Cuban exiles look back on absurdities, tragedy of Bay of Pigs." *Las Vegas Review-Journal* (April 13, 1986).

Sikora, Frank. "Alabama B-26 pilot recounts ill-fated Bay of Pigs invasion." *The Birmingham News* (May 6, 1998).

Slavin, Barbara. "CIA brings spies in from anonymity." *USA Today* (September 18, 1997).

Smith, Jean Edward. "Bay of Pigs: The Unanswered Questions." *The Nation* (April 13, 1964).

"Some Are More Neutral Than Others." *The Montgomery Advertiser* (April 15, 1961).

"The price of military folly. JFK, the CIA and Cuban exiles: A disaster called the Bay of Pigs." *U.S. News & World Report* (April 22, 1996).

Weiner, Tim. "CIA Bares Own Bungling in Bay of Pigs Report." *New York Times* (February 22, 1998).

Weisskopf, M. P. "Motion to Move Doster Trial Denied." *The Montgomery Advertiser* (July 7, 1972).

_____. "U.S. to Drop Cases After Doster Quits." *The Montgomery Advertiser* (August 22, 1972).

"We're 'In' Cuba's Struggle." *The Birmingham News* (April 20, 1961).

Wheeler, Keith. "Hell of a Beating in Cuba." *Life* (April 28, 1961).

Wise, David and Thomas B. Ross. "The Strange Case of the CIA Widows." *Look* (June 30, 1964).

Index